Anonymous

History of the Dewitt Guard, Company A, 50th regiment National Guard, State of New York

Anonymous

History of the Dewitt Guard, Company A, 50th regiment National Guard, State of New York

ISBN/EAN: 9783337416942

Printed in Europe, USA, Canada, Australia, Japan

Cover: Foto ©ninafisch / pixelio.de

More available books at **www.hansebooks.com**

HISTORY

OF THE

DeWitt Guard,

COMPANY A,

50th Regiment National Guard,

STATE OF NEW YORK.

PUBLISHED BY THE COMPANY.

ITHACA, N. Y.:
ANDRUS, McCHAIN & CO., STEAM PRINTERS.
1866

PREFACE.

Our object in giving to the public a full, true, and concise history of Company A, 50th Regiment National Guard, State of New York, better known to the citizens of Ithaca as the De-Witt Guard, is to show as honorable a record as can be produced by any similar organization—so far as the membership of this Company was connected with the army and navy of the United States during the late rebellion. We shall show that the total membership of the Company from the time of its organization, in December, 1851, to the present time, has been two hundred and two, of which eighty-two served either in the army or navy during the war against eighty-eight who did not; twenty-nine names appear on the Company roll, of whom it is not known to the writer whether they were or were not in the army, and nine who died previous to the war. We have undertaken a brief personal history to each, which we believe will be interesting to the reader.

We also wish to show that the Company has been, from the time of its organization to the present, a self-supporting and self-sustaining institution, until recently receiving nothing from the State but arms, and that the individual members have contributed the sum of two thousand seven hundred and twenty dollars and fifty-six cents, to which amount should be added a liberal percentage for disbursements which do not appear on Company records.

We propose to give the name of each member of the DeWitt Guard from its organization, the date of his enlistment, his profession, with such incidents as we think will be of interest to the reader, after which we shall give the history of the Company collectively. There may be those who have belonged to the Company whose names will not appear in these pages. This must be attributed to the fact of their not signing the muster-roll of the Company, as every name there recorded is introduced in the following history.

HISTORY.

ARCH. H. MCNEIL, Merchant, enlisted November 5th, 1851. At the first election of company officers McNeil was chosen second Lieutenant, which position he honorably and creditably filled to the time of his death, which occurred November 28th, 1855. To Lieutenant McNeil the Company were much indebted. To him more than any other one man, belonged the credit of organizing the Company.

He was loved, respected, and honored by both officers and men, and his death caused a breach not easily repaired. Upon receiving intelligence of his death, the Company were immediately called together and the following resolutions unanimously adopted:

Resolved, That in the death of Lieutenant A. H. McNeil the members of this Company have not only lost a commissioned officer in whom a zealous, lively and effective interest for the welfare of the Company always prevailed, but an officer whose military bearing commanded our respect, and a fellow soldier whose conduct and kindness has merited and won our esteem. That we deeply feel his loss, and mourn his untimely departure from our midst,

Resolved, That we tender to the widow and relatives of our deceased officer our sincere condolence in this their great affliction.

Resolved, That we accompany the remains of our late officer to the depot on the morrow, and that a delegation of seven men accompany his remains to the city of Auburn as an escort and attend his funeral.

Resolved, That on all parades we will wear the usual badge of mourning for one year.

At a special meeting held on the return from Auburn of the escort which accompanied the remains of Lieut. A. H. McNeil, and after hearing the report of the officer commanding said escort, the following preamble and resolutions were unanimously adopted:

WHEREAS, An escort from this Company having been delegated to accompany and perform the last sad duties over the remains of our esteemed friend, Lieut. A. H. McNeil, at Auburn, and while there having met with reception and attention which ever characterize the true and tried friend and soldier, be it therefore

Resolved, That to General Segoin and Colonel Jenkins, and their respective staffs, to the Auburn City Guard, Willard Guard, and to the delegation from other Companies, we as a Company return them our sincere and heartfelt thanks for the manner in which they cared for them, and the kindness with which they were every where greeted by them while there, and in the admirable arrangements for the funeral made at such short notice, and for the cheerful and handsome manner in which they were carried out; gratified as we are, words can only attempt a description of our feelings of the manner in which they alleviated our sorrows in the burial of our dead. And although the deceased had not resided among them for years, yet like us they appreciated his many virtues and, remembered his uniform kindness to all, and when they but learned of his decease, their tears mingled with ours at our irreparable loss.

Resolved, That in future, should it be possible for us to repay them in any manner that it will be forthcoming, feeling, as we do, that no sacrifice will be too great in attempting a return of their kindness in the hour of our affliction, and as individuals, as citizens and as soldiers, we hope that the choicest of Heaven's blessings may be theirs, and that their respective staffs and Companies may ever meet with prosperity.

GEORGE H. COLLINS, Merchant, enlisted November 5th, 1851. Mr. Collins was permitted to serve but a short time as a member of the Company, as he was selected by the Colonel and commissioned Adjutant of the Regiment, which position he held for many years. Changing his residence to the city of New York, his connection with the 50th Regiment was dissolved.

BEN. B. WILCOX, Hotel keeper, enlisted November 5th, 1851. Served with the Company but a short time; removed to Owego; was for a time proprietor of the Ah-Wa-Ga House, but more recently of a hotel at Saratoga Springs.

WILLIAM M. SMITH, Brewer, enlisted November 5th, 1851. Served but a short time.

H. F. RANDOLPH, Shoe Merchant, enlisted November 5th, 1851. Mr. Randolph had more than served his time, and reached the rank of Captain, in the old militia before joining this organization. He was an officer of no common attainments—prompt, active and generous. The interest he had always manifested, and now felt, in military matters, compelled him to join this new enterprise; he enlisted as a private, and is to this day an honorary member of the Company. He has accompanied them on many an excursion, and is always invested with the command of the honorary members. The Captain has now attained the age of sixty-three years, and is still as smart, hale and hearty as a lad of sixteen.

J. C. McWHORTER, Merchant, enlisted November 5th, 1851. Remained but a short time with the Company, but the soul-stirring strains of music, as rendered by him on the snare drum while he was a member, will long be remembered by those associated with him during his short military experience.

FRED. S. LAMOUREUX, Musician, enlisted November 5th, 1851. Was a very valuable member for a very short time; for while resting from the fatigue of drill, Lamoureux always furnished the music for the *light foot* portion of the Company.

WILLIAM S. ALLEN, Carpenter, enlisted November 6th, 1851. Was a faithful and exemplary member for a few years, and undoubtedly his connection with this Company gave him the position he has honorably filled since his removal from us—that of policeman in New York city. He was consequently transferred as Sergeant from this Company to Sergeant of police in that city.

K. MORRIS, Clothing Merchant, enlisted November 7th, 1851. Served but a short time.

S. NEWMARK, Clothing Merchant, enlisted November 10th, 1851. Served faithfully for a short time and was granted an honorable discharge.

J. G. CONRAD, Clerk, enlisted November 8th, 1851. Mr. Conrad faithfully performed the duties of a member of this Company for a short time.

L. R. KING, Merchant, enlisted November 9th, 1851. At the time of the organization of the Company, Mr. King was elected fourth Sergeant, and by promotion filled each office up to first Lieutenant, and was in command of the Company for some time. Lieutenant King, by his kind and pleasing way, and the interest he ever manifested in the welfare of the Company, commanded the respect and admiration of every man who served under him. He held the commission of first Lieutenant from May 28th, 1856, to August 25th, 1862. Upon his resignation being accepted, he was voted an honorary membership for life. He is one of the enterprising firm of Treman, King & Co., large manufacturers. We believe that Mr. King can look back upon the years spent in the DeWitt Guard as not altogether unprofitable.

W. B. HATFIELD, Clerk, enlisted November 15th, 1851. Mr. Hatfield was a good soldier; was in the employ of L. H. Culver, Esq.; retained his connection with the Company and his employer until his removal to the West.

SPENCE SPENCER, Book Merchant, enlisted November 15th, 1851. Retained his membership but a short time, but with the liberality which was always a prominent characteristic of Mr. Spencer, he donated to the Company a complete uniform, which is the first recorded gift made to the DeWitt Guard. He is still a citizen of Ithaca, and has of late attached no small degree of honor to his name by publishing the book entitled, "The Scenery of Ithaca."

L. MILLSPAUGH, dealer in Harness, Trunks, &c., enlisted November 15th, 1851. Mr. Millspaugh was an old soldier before joining this Company, having held the commission of Lieut. Colonel in the old militia, issued by Gov. Seward in 1842; but feeling a deep interest in the organization of a new Company, enlisted as a private. On the 29th day of January, 1852, he was elected first Corporal, which position he held but a short time, as he was gradually promoted until he had filled nearly all the grades of non-commissioned offices. He always declined accepting a commission, and when it seemed to be the unanimous wish of the Company, his prompt reply was "No." He continued an invaluable member until long after he had served his time, (seven years,) when he was granted an honorable discharge. Our friend, by his emphatic "No," has not been as successful, however, in a political way, he having repeatedly been called to fill civil offices of honor and trust;

and by his being re-elected to most of the offices he has held, is in itself sufficient to show his standing in the community in which he lives. Whether all this would have been so, had he never joined the DeWitt Guard, we leave for a discriminating public to judge.

J. B. TERRY, Merchant, enlisted November 15th, 1851. Mr. Terry filled the office of Secretary of the Company for the first two years of its existence. He was a good soldier, an exemplary and respected citizen, and the community generally mourned his loss when he was removed by death.

JEROME ROWE, Lawyer, enlisted November 18th, 1851. Some unhappy misunderstanding caused the withdrawal of Mr. Rowe from the Company during the early part of its history. He was untiring in his endeavors to establish the organization, and the same energy and devotion which he displayed at that time, has followed him thus far through life. He filled the office of Special County Judge of Tompkins County, with honor to himself and perfect satisfaction to the people. He entered the army of the United States April 1st, 1861, was commissioned Captain of Company A, 32d New York volunteers, same date, and served as such one year.

Hugh McDonald, enlisted November 18th, 1851. Was elected Orderly Sergeant Dec. 31st of the same year, which position he filled as long as he was a resident of the village. McDonald was a soldier of much experience, having served in the Mexican war, where he became perfectly familiar with the duties pertaining to the soldier in the field. As a drill-master he was not excelled, and under his instruction the Company soon became very proficient in the manual of arms, and school of the soldier and Company. At the outbreak of the Rebellion he enlisted in a Pennsylvania Regiment, was very soon promoted to Captain, and again to Major. We should be glad to give a full history of his life through the war, but have been unable to obtain it. This much we can say, he was a patriotic citizen, a true soldier, and a faithful officer.

N. H. Curtis, Upholsterer, enlisted November 19th, 1851. Was long connected with the Company; filled the posts of Corporal and Sergeant. After a long residence in our village, he removed to the West, where he survived but a few years.

Daniel Place, Jeweler, enlisted November ―― 1851. Mr. Place joined the Company in order that the number required by law might be secured, so as to enable them to proceed with the election of officers. He never served as an active member.

Lucius F. Pease, Painter, enlisted November 20th, 1851. Mr. Pease well and faithfully performed the duties required of him as a member of the DeWitt Guard for the full term of his enlistment, (seven years,) and was granted an honorable discharge. He is still living in Ithaca, an industrious mechanic, and a good citizen.

Christopher Whaley, Druggist, enlisted November 21, 1851. Was discharged on Surgeon's certificate soon after his enlistment.

William Glenny, Clerk, enlisted November 21st, 1851. December 31st was elected fourth Corporal; March 3d, 1853, was elected Secretary, which office he most creditably filled, as the records of the Company show, up to January, 1857; was elected fourth Sergeant Jan. 14th, 1857; May 17th, 1861, second Sergeant, which office he held at the time of his enlistment in the United States army.

The subject of this sketch reflects great credit

upon the Company to which he formerly belonged, and in the perilous hour honored his constituency, as well as himself, to a degree unparalelled in the history of the Rebellion. Having in his former life been a warm and ardent supporter of the inalienable rights of man, and an exponent of a free government, the first attempt by traitors to destroy its fair fabric, bought by the blood of our fathers, and to trample under foot the time-honored and beloved emblem of our free and independent nationality, so enraged his sense of right and justice, that he at once expressed his determination to fulfill his public declarations to the effect, that when traitors should thrust the bayonet at the nation's life, he would be found among those who were willing to peril their lives in its defence.

Being met with opposition and the remonstrance of friends, that there were single men, and those more inured to hardship, sufficient for the emergency, whose duty it was to go first, his plans were for a time delayed, and until a second or third reverse of our arms, when he could no longer be restrained, went earnestly at work, and by his persistent efforts succeeded in raising a sufficient number of volunteers for the basis of a Company; which, by authority of the commandant of the Elmira rendezvous, in accordance with orders from the Adjutant General of the State, was organized at Ithaca Sept. 10th, 1861, and by him conducted to Elmira, where, by a unanimous vote of the Company, he was elected its Captain, and so commissioned by Gov. Seymour, commission bearing date Sept. 13th, 1861.

Captain Glenny then went earnestly at work and recruited his Company to the minimum standard, and by vote of its members united its destinies with the 64th Regiment N. Y. Volunteers, commanded by Col. Thomas J. Parker.

On the 10th of December the Regiment moved to Washington, and a month later crossed the Potomac and camped with the main army three miles west of Alexandria, and was brigaded under General O. O. Howard, who commanded the first Brigade, first Division, second Corps. Early in the spring of 1862, the Brigade moved one week in advance of the main army for the purpose of repairing the Orange & Alexandria Railroad. A short distance beyond Fairfax Station signs of the enemy were discovered, and for safety to the command, two Companies from the 64th, under command of Captain Glenny, (his own being one of the number) were sent some considerable distance to the front as an extreme outpost. Here the first blood of the opening campaign was drawn by shooting a rebel scout by one of Captain Glenny's men.

The main army soon after advanced to the famous fields of Manassas, but only to find the enemy beating a hasty retreat, leaving every conceivable ruin in their track.

At this juncture the army changed its base to the Peninsula and Chickahominy swamps, where, after the siege of Yorktown, and on the first of June, was fought the terrific battle of Fair Oaks, in which Captain Glenny, while leading his men in a charge, received a wound, which, for a time, was thought to be mortal, a minnie ball passing through his left shoulder.

In about two months he again returned to his command, but so disabled that he was detached on recruiting service and stationed at Elmira; after which he returned to the army, and after nearly another year's campaign, was, in accordance with orders, again detached at Elmira on service connected with the draft. After being relieved from this duty, he rejoined his command, with which he served until the close of the war.

Owing to circumstances beyond his control, he served near two and a half years as Captain without promotion, after which in rapid succession he received the different grades of Major, Lieut. Colonel and Colonel, but was unable to muster into the latter grade by reason of insufficiency of numbers in the Regiment. This was, however, in part recompensed for, as after the smoke of battle and the clash of arms had ceased, and honors were conferred upon " whom honor was due," Captain Glenny had two grades by brevet conferred upon him by the President, that of Brevet Colonel and Brevet Brigadier General, for gallant and meritorious services—honors which he modestly and unassumingly wears, but of which he may justly be proud.

From the time of his entry into the service until the close of the war, near four years, (except while suffering from wounds and on detached service,) General Glenny fought traitors with unrelenting fidelity to principle and the inalienable rights of man.

The number of decisive battles of which he may claim to be hero, and in which he had the honor to bare his breast to the bayonet and bullet, are twenty-two ; six of them being bayonet charges and direct assaults upon the enemy and their fortifications. Among the principal of these battles may be placed Fair Oaks, Chancellorville, Gettysburg, Po River, Wilderness, Spottsylvania, Coal Harbor, Deep Bottom, Petersburg, Gravelly Run, Southside Road, Farmville, Reams Station, &c. The Regiment fought in upwards of thirty-three. General Glenny's superior officers being wounded, he was invested with the command of the Regiment on the battle-field of Spottsylvania, which command he retained until the close of the war, except at different periods, by seniority of rank, he commanded a Brigade. At the battle of Ream's Station he took command of the Brigade which he retained for some considerable time, as so fierce had been the campaign that but one other field officer was left for duty in the Brigade comprising seven Regiments. Had we time and space, many acts of personal bravery and valorous deeds might be accredited to this officer during his brief career of warfare, as owing to his known integrity of character and ability, superior officers frequently selected him to fill posts of great danger.

General Glenny's command has the honor of

being the first infantry troops upon the Southside Railroad, also of making the last charge upon the enemy at Farmville, April 7th, 1865.

Two or three circumstances of peculiar interest, showing the morals of this officer, may not be inappropriate, and in a degree indicate his decision of character and fidelity to his untarnished reputation and walks of private life.

In the latter part of May, 1862, and just prior to the battle of Fair Oaks, by orders of General McClellan, the first ration of whiskey was issued to the troops. This being incompatible with the principles of General Glenny, he at once called his men in line, and stated that he believed the new element just introduced in the army was destructive of its best interests, prejudicial to its health, efficiency and discipline, and rather than stultify his conscience by being responsible for its issue, he would suffer himself to be cashiered for disobedience of orders. His position having been defined, the question was submitted to the Company, which, by a unanimous vote, rejected the whiskey. During the day General Howard, who by some means had become acquainted with the facts, at once dispatched one of his aids with a book, his compliments and a message, to General Glenny, to the effect that he was the only officer in the Brigade who had taken that position, and was gratified to know he had one under his command who had sufficient moral courage to take so exalted a stand.

At Chancellorville, where the Union army met with temporary defeat, this Regiment made one of the most gallant stands of any during the war. It held its position and repulsed five successive charges made by the enemy under cover of their artillery. The enemy, a few minutes later, succeeded in turning the right of our lines, when orders were sent to General Glenny to withdraw his men immediately, which he did successfully under a galling fire, and just as the enemy were closing in upon him from front and rear in the form of a pair of shears.

Again at Po River, the Regiment was hastily thrown out as a skirmish line. Owing to emergencies the main army were obliged to change position so suddenly, that there was no time to withdraw or notify the skirmish line of their perilous position; and the only alternative was to leave them to their fate. It was not until some two hours later, when mistrusting all was not right, and finding the main army had left the position a few hours previously taken up, it was decided at once to make desperate efforts to extricate the Regiment, which was found to be surrounded on three sides, and the fourth fast closing in, which was accomplished with but slight loss. This was a prominent trait in General Glenny's character, to always hazard life rather than be a prisoner in the hands of traitors, whom he looked upon with contempt and scorn.

In the last charge made by the Regiment, or any of the army, at Farmville, April 7th, 1865, General Glenny lost fourteen men, and one officer of the rank of Captain. The latter finding himself mortally wounded, and having been rather a reckless young man, at once became alarmed with reference to his future state. While lying on the field, he called General Glenny, (then Colonel,) took him by the hand, and as soon as he could gather sufficient strength to speak, says, " Colonel, can you pray?" When answered in the affirmative he said, " I have got to die and am unprepared." In compliance with his request, General Glenny knelt by his side in prayer; but as missiles of death were flying on every hand, and the enemy opening an increasing fire, which required him to watch as well as pray, and to attend to the living as well as the dying, he at once ordered the Captain carried to the rear, where he soon died, leaving good evidence that he had found spiritual relief.

This was the closing drama of the war, as two days after General Lee surrendered the rebel army of Northern Virginia to General Grant. The Union army soon after returned to Washington and vicinity, where, by different commands, they were mustered out of service. The 64th proceeded to Elmira, where it received final pay and discharge July 24th, 1865. Thus ended near four years of warfare with General Glenny; he being the only officer who went out as such who returned with the Regiment.

The General is now engaged in the mercantile trade, and located in the store formerly occupied by John Kendall, Esq., and is carrying on a very successful and profitable trade.

STEPHEN BREWER, Saddles, Harness, &c., enlisted November 21st, 1851. Mr. Brewer was a good soldier; his membership with the Company was soon dissolved by his removal to Cortland village, where, like his professional broth-

or Millspaugh, he has held many offices of trust and honor, among which was County Judge of Cortland county.

F. K. ANDRUS, Bookseller, &c., enlisted November 21st, 1851. Mr. Andrus has answered to his name as fourth, third, second and first Corporal, and fifth, fourth, third and second Sergeants. Was one of the most active members of the Company during the whole seven years, and over, of his membership. We find but very few meetings or drills of the Company that he is not marked present. He was a thorough soldier, never satisfied with half knowing how. His motto was, "Excelsior." No member who served while Sergeant Andrus was connected with the Company, will ever forget him; always good-natured and cheerful, inclined to look on the bright and never on the dark side of the picture; and during times in the history of the Company, when many were despondent, and the future looked any thing but encouraging, he was always with a cheerful heart and a ready hand, willing to contribute in whatever way was necessary to raise the standard of the Company; and we believe whatever he undertook he succeeded in accomplishing. Mr. Andrus is now one of the firm of Andrus, McChain & Co., probably the largest Paper Manufacturers in Western New York; and very many of our citizens and distinguished visitors from abroad, can testify to his politeness and urbanity in showing them through their large manufactory at Fall Creek.

CHARLES CLAPP, Painter, enlisted November 21st, 1851. Mr. Clapp, at his own request, was granted a discharge soon after his enlistment. His military ardor was in no degree dampened, however, as will be seen from the following: He enlisted in the United States army December 30th, 1863, in Company M, 21st New York Cavalry, in which he served eighteen months; was engaged in the battle of New Market, and in the reserve at Cedar Creek. Mr. Clapp also had two sons in the army. He was particularly distinguished for his Good Samaritan kindness, as many of his comrades can testify. Having some knowledge of medicine, he imparted the all-healing balm to those about him who were sick or wounded.

E. C. FULLER, Painter, enlisted November 21st, 1851. He filled the offices of Corporal and Sergeant; was a good soldier, a faithful officer, and a skilled artisan.

WILLIAM V. BRUYN, Lawyer, enlisted November 21st, 1851. Immediately upon his joining the Company he was elected first Lieutenant, which commission he held until his removal to Syracuse. He was a man of talents and fine accomplishments, which, combined with his gentlemanly bearing, made an officer of which the Company were at all times proud. He was once District Attorney of Tompkins county, and is now engaged in his profession in the city of Syracuse, where he meets with that success he so richly merits.

LOREN DAY, wholesale Liquor dealer, enlisted November 21st, 1851. Mr. Day, we believe, never served as a member but a short time, if at all. His connection, however, with this or any other institution, would be an honor to it. He is one of the most quiet, still one of the best, citizens of our village. He has been very successful in business, which may be credited to his strict attention and uncompromising honesty.

WILLIAM M. CULVER, dealer in Hats, Caps and Furs, enlisted November 22d, 1851. Served but a short time, a worthy member, and was honorably discharged. He is still successfully engaged in the above business.

Theodore A. Hanmer, Clerk, enlisted November 24th, 1851. Very soon after enlistment he removed to a Southern State, where he still resides.

Philip J. Partenheimer, Cashier Tompkins County Bank, enlisted November 25th, 1851. We often hear it said there is no man but has his enemies; this may be the rule, we will produce the exception.

At the first election of Company A, held in December, 1851, Mr. Partenheimer was unanimously elected their Captain, which commission he held until August 25th, 1862—over ten years. Nearly two hundred men served under him while Captain of this Company, by each of which he was not only respected and honored as their commanding officer, but as a citizen and gentleman. Few officers ever had the confidence, respect and esteem of his command as did Captain Partenheimer. Very likely some were at times dissatisfied with his rulings; soon, however, his sound judgment was apparent, and his decisions perfectly satisfactory to all. When necessary he was stern, but always kind and forgiving. When he gave a command, his men knew it must be promptly and correctly executed. His generosity was only exceeded (so far as his Company was concerned) by his desire to have his gifts unknown to the members or others, and if it could be known how much he had paid for the use and improvement of his Company, a very considerable sum could be added to the amount of disbursements spoken of in the preface of this record.

Captain Partenheimer's first business engagement was with S. B. Munn, Jr., of this village. His clerkship was of short duration, however, as his superior talent as an accountant was soon displayed, and he made his second engagement with the Tompkins County Bank as book-keeper. With this situation the same remarks are applicable as to the clerkship; he was soon promoted to the position of Teller of the same institution, and later to Cashier, which office he still holds. His various and rapid promotions in the Bank were not equal, however, to the demands made upon him by his fellow citizens. To show his popularity, we mention some of the civil offices he has filled: Town Clerk, Notary Public, Trustee of the village, President of same repeatedly, Chief Engineer of the Fire Department for many years in succession, and also served his town in the Board of Supervisors of Tompkins county. Each of the above mentioned offices he has filled with honor to himself, and for us to say with satisfaction to the people, would be superfluous. It is worthy of note, that Captain Partenheimer never was ambitious for office; that all the offices he has filled, both civil and military, have been thrust upon him; and it is proverbial in his case, that he has in the most positive and peremptory manner, declined many honors that the community have endeavored to heap upon him. He is, most emphatically, a self-made man; and to his own personal exertions the public are indebted for a man of sterling worth and vast usefulness.

PHILIP STEPHENS, Butcher, enlisted November 25th, 1851. Mr. Stephens was one of the best soldiers of the DeWitt Guard; and not only this, but one of the most valuable men for the Company. He would allow nothing to prevent his attendance at the drills and meetings, where he always took an active part, as he also did in the general welfare of the Company. His purse was always open to contribute to any object that had in view the advancement of the institution. He creditably filled most of the non-commissioned offices; enjoyed being a soldier, and the Company enjoyed him as such. Mr. Stephens has been very successful in his business enterprises, and has built up a reputation throughout the State. The epicure of New York city as well as Chicago, satisfies his taste with luxuries provided by Stephens in the way of choice meats. Mr. Stephens has recently purchased one of the most beautiful building sites in our village, and intends soon building a handsome and capacious dwelling.

A. PHILLIPS, Merchant Tailor, enlisted November 25th, 1851. Mr. Phillips remained with the Company but a short time, and upon his retiring therefrom, presented them with a new uniform complete. It has always been the pleasure of Mr. Phillips to lend his influence for the benefit of the Company, and has furnished in the person of his son a most worthy and valuable member.

JOHN S. VANLIEW, Clerk, enlisted November 29th, 1851. Removed from the district soon after joining the Company.

A. G. THOMPSON, enlisted November 29th, 1851. With the history of Mr. Thompson the writer is not acquainted.

JOHN RANDOLPH, Mason, enlisted December 1st, 1851. Was an excellent member for some years; his tall and commanding form, his precise and measured step and general bearing, fitted him for a first-class soldier. He removed to Michigan about 1858. Joining a Michigan Regiment, he entered the United States army in 1861; was commissioned as Captain soon after his enlistment, and for meritorious conduct was promoted to Major. He was a brave soldier and a courageous officer. He died soon after honorably serving the time of his enlistment, from disease contracted while in the service.

We copy the following to show the esteem in which he was held by his command:

"MINER'S HILL, VA., November 18th, 1861.

We, the undersigned, members of Company D, (Barry Guard,) 4th Michigan Volunteers, in testimony of our high appreciation of our beloved Captain, John Randolph, for his uniform urbanity to, and kind treatment of, his Company, and for his ability as an officer, do hereby present him with the accompanying slight memento of our highest regard.

J. N. Hall, E. S. Baldwin, G. G. Mowry, and ninety-seven other members of the Company."

SPEECH OF MAJOR BARRY.

"Captain Randolph: I have been commissioned by the members of Company D, (Barry Guard,) under your command, to present you in their behalf this beautiful sword and belt, in testimony of their high appreciation of your uniform urbanity to, and kind treatment of, your Company, and of your ability as an officer.

While I feel honored in being the medium of communication between the Company (which, among all others, possesses my highest affection) and yourself, I can refer with pride to this testimonial as conclusive evidence, not only of your high qualities as an officer, but also the kindness of your heart.

Captain, I commit this sword to your keeping in confidence, that possessing those qualities as an officer and a man, you will never suffer it to be dishonored."

RESPONSE OF CAPTAIN RANDOLPH.

"Major Barry: No words that I may speak can express my feelings on this occasion. But a few days ago I left behind me a brave band of tried and true men, whose warm expressions of concern for my safety and speedy return scarcely die away in the distance, ere I am followed by a more substantial token of their esteem for me, and kindness of heart, in the shape of this beautiful sword. Coming, as it does, unexpectedly and in so delicate a way, it is not a wonder that my eye should express a feeling that is foreign to my heart. We are bound together in a brotherhood, by ties more binding and endearing than those which make up friendship in civil life. With the same old flag floating over us, sharing a common and imminent danger perpetually about us, with the thousand other incidental and reciprocal acts of courtesy attending well ordered camp-life, it would be strange if we did not become brothers in feeling, as well as in action. As I felt a gladness a few days ago, when departing from camp on a short furlough to visit my many friends here, so now on returning I feel my heart bound at the thought that I shall soon hear the cheers of comrads, and feel the warm grasp of their stout hands. We have ever remembered and looked upon you, Major Barry, as the father of our Company, and feel proud that we bear the name of the Barry Guard. When the boom of the gun of treason first rolled through the land, and the harsh voice of actual war broke upon the startled ears of our peaceful and happy people, your voice called us together, gave our zeal direction, and cooled our excitement to concentrated action; and not one of us will ever cease to regret that other duties prevented your accompanying us in a cause we all know has your whole heart and sympathy. This splendid gift, then, comes to me with double effect. It is like the donation of brothers tendered by the hand of a father, and so I receive it. And I here swear never to dishonor the blade nor disgrace the donors, but whenever I can strike a blow for the right, for our cause, for our flag and the Union, it shall leap from the scabbard, and God helping me, shall not be again sheathed while this right arm can strike a blow, or victory remains uncertain."

SHERMAN K. HALL, Grocer, enlisted December 2d, 1851. Remained with the Company but a short time.

WILLIAM O. BRYAN, Shoemaker, enlisted December 2d, 1851. Removed from town very soon after enlistment; is now engaged in the Drug and Medicine trade of the West.

F. A. PARTENHEIMER, proprietor of the "Continental Boot and Shoe Store." A strong desire to become a military gentleman led Mr. Partenheimer to enlist in the militia of the State, which he did January 1st, 1852, when he found that he possessed all the proper qualifications of a good soldier. Undoubtedly, however, these necessary qualifications were more apparent to others than himself, as he was soon elected Corporal, from which he was promoted to Sergeant, and most worthily did he fill his office, until having served his seven years he was granted an honorable discharge. Our sincere regrets are extended to any Company which does not number among its members at least one man like Sergeant Partenheimer. A more true and devoted soldier never existed; but upon him nature had bestowed a great deal more than the ordinary amount of original wit; and at times, when not on duty, our Sergeant would furnish innocent fun for a Regiment. At Camp Burnett, Sept. 1859, he was the life of the camp, and many of his jokes are not, to this day, forgotten.

It gives us pleasure to state, that now Mr. Partenheimer is sole proprietor of one of our most successful and enterprising Boot and Shoe manufactories, and is receiving that portion of public patronage which he merits.

CHARLES F. BLOOD, Merchant Tailor, enlisted January 1st, 1852. In joining this Company, Mr. Blood's first and greatest ambition was to become a thorough soldier, which object he successfully accomplished we shall proceed to show.

Very soon after becoming a member of the Company, he was elected their standard-bearer. His strong desire to become familiar with all the rudiments, and to become perfect, not only in the school of the soldier, but also of the Company and Battalion, led him to devote but little time to the duties of his new office. So anxious was he to learn, that with the Tactics for his drill-master, and a borrowed gun for an assistant, he would by himself combine the theoretical with the practical. We say without fear of contradiction, that to-day a man more conversant with the theory and practice of the science of military, cannot be found.

The 28th of May, 1856, he was elected and commissioned second Lieutenant, which office he filled until August 25th, 1862, at which time he was elected Captain. As a commanding officer Captain Blood could not be excelled. The time he had so studiously devoted in the earlier part of his military career to this object, he now discovered was of great use to him. Combine with this knowledge his splendid voice and fine military carriage, he was an officer of which his men were at all times proud.

When the Company volunteered and were mustered into the United States service, Captain Blood accompanied them; and through his exertions they obtained a very desirable position in the 58th Regiment National Guard. It was his chief and constant aim to see that his men were at all times comfortable, and to see that they, as United States soldiers, had all they were entitled to.

Very soon after joining the army, Captain Blood was detailed from his Company and commissioned one of the court-martial of the Department of New York, before which court was transacted a large amount of business. The compliments that were bestowed upon Captain Blood as a member of this court, by the Division and Post Commanders, and by other members of the court, must, indeed, have been very flattering to him. In his decisions (not one of which were ever set aside or annulled) he was prompt and discriminating, always tempering his judgment with that amount of clemency which he considered was best for the Government he represented, and for the unfortunate delinquents who appeared before him.

Notwithstanding he was so much of the time seperated from his command, still he endeavored to be in camp with them every night, and a large portion of the time messed with them.

Captain Blood, as every person knows who is acquainted with him, was a strictly conscientious man, and still he always enjoyed the sports and harmless amusements of his men in camp, and at all proper times and occasions would join with them. It is needless for us to say, that each member of his Company became very much attached to him, not one of which but would have sacrificed their all for his comfort.

His door was always open and he was at all times glad to see his men, and his tent was Company Head-Quarters *indeed*. It was the remark of very many officers and others who visited Elmira during encampment of this Company, that Captain Blood was the most accomplished officer, and commanded the best Company of men, that assisted in garrisoning that post during the war.

The Captain always attended the religious services of the Regiment, and by this means exerted a beneficial influence over his men. His example was always that of an uncompromising christian, as well as a good soldier and true patriot.

Immediately following the Elmira campaign, Captain Blood was elected and commisioned Lieutenant Colonel of the 50th Regiment National Guard, and now holds that commission.

In this instance we see a private of Company A, by various promotions, reach the rank second in command of the Regiment, and undoubtedly in a short time will be in full command. No officer is more worthy the honor than Colonel Blood.

In civil life he is none the less honored, having filled public offices with equal success.

He has been not only a good soldier, a respected Lieutenant, honored Captain and esteemed Colonel, but is a citizen of the highest standing and respected by every one.

H. J. WILSON, Painter, enlisted January 1st, 1852. Mr. Wilson served his full time and received an honorable discharge as a soldier, but is still connected with the Regiment as a musician. It is the strong desire of every member of the Company, as well as of the Regiment, that his membership may be continued yet many years. Our excellent Band, without Wilson, would be like tinkling brass—of uncertain sound. The rich, full and expressive tones rendered by him on his powerful Tuba, fully prove him to be a musician of no ordinary talent.

JACOB SAGER, Clerk, enlisted January 1st, 1852. Was Company musician, which position he filled until his removal from the District. He was not only a good musician, but a gentleman.

CLARK WILSON, Machinist, enlisted January —, 1852. Mr. Wilson was Company drummer for a time, but preferring a gun to a drum, took his place in the ranks; served some time; is now Chief Engineer on Seneca Lake.

HORACE ROOT, Brewer, enlisted March 17th, 1852. Mr. Root was always promptly on hand at the drills and meetings of the Company while a member. The record does not show how long he was connected with the Company; our recollection is some three years.

CALEB BABCOCK, enlisted March 17th, 1852. His membership was short; very soon after becoming a member he left the place. He is now an officer on one of the New York and Liverpool Line of Steamers.

A. J. TERRY, Tobacconist, enlisted May 15th, 1852. Mr. Terry was a good member of the Company and a good citizen. He died a few years ago, after suffering the most excrutiating torture of acute rheumatism.

JAMES C. McCLUNE, Lawyer, enlisted June 3d, 1852. Mr. McClune always evinced the greatest interest in the welfare of the Company; he was one of its best workers, was a first-class soldier, and was soon elected Corporal from which he was promoted to Sergeant, which office he held until November 29th, 1856, when he was removed by death. Upon receiving intelligence of his death a special meeting was called, when the following preamble and resolutions, offered by Lieut. King, were unanimously adopted:

WHEREAS, The Supreme Ruler of the Universe has, in the exercise of His power and wisdom, seen fit to remove from our midst our esteemed friend and fellow soldier, Sergeant James C. McClune, therefore be it

Resolved, That we receive the sad bereavement as a mandate from Him who doeth all things well.

Resolved, That we offer our sincere and heartfelt condolence to the sorrowing family of the deceased, and we assure them that we will ever revere the memory of their son and brother.

Resolved, That as a mark of our respect for the character of our deceased comrad, we will attend his funeral, and escort his remains to their last resting place with military honors.

Resolved, That we wear the usual badge of mourning for the space of six months.

Resolved, That a copy of these resolutions, signed by the Chairman and Secretary, be presented to the family of the deceased, and published in the village papers.

P. J. PARTENHEIMER, *Captain.*

WILLIAM GLENNY, *Sec'y.*

JAMES H. GREENLY, Merchant, enlisted June 3d, 1852. Mr. Greenly was in every respect a most estimable man, and as a soldier he had no superior. Always manifested a lively interest in whatever conduced to the benefit of the organization. He filled all the grades of non-commissioned offices; was Orderly Sergeant at the time he removed from us. No member ever left, carrying with him more well wishes and kind regards, than Sergeant James H. Greenly. Success and prosperity attend him ever in all his undertakings.

JACOB WARSHASKI, Clothing Merchant, enlisted July 1st, 1852. Was a faithful and worthy member for a few years. Upon changing his residence was granted an honorable discharge.

MAJOR A. O. SHAW, Blacksmith. To name a day as the one on which the Major enlisted, is for us an impossibility, and we think it would be too much of a task for him, even, to find out the exact year, say nothing about the day. Suffice it to say, he has been honored with the title of Major from the earliest recollection of the writer. He has seen the time when he had command of more musicians alone than this Company at any one time ever numbered as members. He always enjoyed being a military man, and we believe there could be no greater pleasure for the Major to-day, than to head a column of a few hundred men and march through the streets of Ithaca, as he has done in years gone by. He has received three honorable discharges, each being granted by reason of the expiration of his term of service. This would give the Major twenty-one years in the service, and how much he overran on time on each of the discharges, we doubt if he knows. At all events he was a member of the DeWitt Guard when the writer joined, (which was in 1855,) and served until last year before he received his last discharge.

He has always been, and is to-day, one of the

most accommodating military men of our acquaintance. At any time the Company would like to have him turn out with them, he is always ready, and invariably refuses a single dime compensation. The Major has the respect, not only of the Company with which he has so long served, but of the whole community. As a citizen, his politeness and gentlemanly conduct attracts the attention of every person who meets him; and the various positions he has so long and creditably filled, is sufficient to show that he is properly appreciated by the community in which he resides.

MOSES R. WRIGHT, Lawyer, enlisted July 8th, 1852. Was connected with the Company but a short time; was a man of fine talent, and a lawyer of great ability. He died in this village June 6th, 1855.

L. S. BLUE, Boot and Shoe Merchant, enlisted July 8th, 1852. Mr. Blue served but a short time. Is now a resident of New York city.

JOHN PAGE, Shoemaker, enlisted July 12th, 1852. His membership was short.

D. M. OLTZ, Carpenter, enlisted June 23d, 1853. Was a good soldier and a good member of the Company; served for some time. His membership was dissolved by his removal to Canada.

J. B. HAMMOND, Jeweler, enlisted June 23d, 1853. Served faithfully as Company bugler until his removal to St. Louis.

MELVILLE WILKINSON, Clerk, enlisted July 4th, 1853. Was a good soldier while connected with the Company, and a better one after leaving it. He removed from the district after a membership of one or two years. Upon the breaking out of the war he enlisted in the 23d New York Volunteers; was soon commissioned Lieutenant; served his time; volunteered the second time, and was elected Captain in the 107th New York Volunteers. He was a brave and true officer; was engaged in many battles; was transferred to the Veteran Reserve Corps; afterwards held a prominent position upon the staff of General Coxe, who commanded the Department of Ohio. At the close of the war he devoted his time to preparing himself for the ministry, and is now an Episcopal clergyman, located in Ohio.

THOMAS J. PHILLIPS, Miller. (Date of enlistment not recorded.) Mr. Phillips was no ordinary soldier, as he most conclusively proved to a Bank President at the Seneca Falls encampment. He was always careful to know what his duty was, and then he was going to do it, let the consequences be what they might. He was always good natured, perfectly happy, and was poor society for those troubled with the *blues.* Never wanted much to do with a person who did not feel as good as himself. Was worth at the encampment spoken of above, more than some whole Companies. Had the advantages of an early education and good bringing up, used to living well at home, and believed in living well in camp—*and did.* No person, although he might be President of all the Banks in Hungary, could pass the line when he was the sentinel. He was athletic, not only in person but in mind, and too much good cannot be said of him as a soldier and a citizen. The Company sustained a severe loss when Mr. Phillips removed from among them, and became the proprietor of the Danby Spring Mills.

WILLIAM H. BROWN, Grocer, enlisted July 28th, 1853. Mr. Brown served his full time and received an honorable discharge. He always felt a deep interest in the welfare of the Company; particularly prompt to meet all the demands made upon him; always gave cheerfully, and has in many instances paid for others who could illy afford to pay for themselves; was always careful to have no one know that he paid obligations other than his own; always present at the drills and meetings of the Company, and altogether Mr. Brown was one of the *solid men* of the Company. He has acted as Company Sutler at a number of encampments, and in this capacity has given the most perfect satisfaction.

LEONARD STODDARD, Carriage Maker, enlisted July 28th, 1853. His membership was short —removing from the district soon after joining. He was employed in the extensive establishment of William S. Hoyt, Esq., the largest carriage manufacturer in Western New York.

SAMUEL STODDARD, Wool and Leather Merchant, enlisted June 29th, 1854.

In the DeWitt Guard, as well as in every other organization or association with which Mr. Stoddard has been connected, he was, as he would term his best grade of wool, super extra. He was an old militiaman when he joined this Company, and had improved all the advantages to be derived from the Old Guard, which in an eminent degree qualified him for a good soldier in this, then new, Company. A peculiar trait in the military character of Mr. Stoddard was, he invariably attended the drills and meetings of the Company. Consider, with this fact, the large business carried on by him, which one would suppose would require his undivided time and attention, and we find he must have sacrificed a good deal for the interest he felt in this Company. He would forego other enjoyments for the sake of attending the weekly drills in which he took much pleasure, believing that this exercise was of vast good to him. He became a very proficient soldier; never would accept office of any kind, though besought with tears; his highest ambition was to be a *good* high private; was one of the most liberal men in the Company, always contributing freely, and many times more than his proportion; was always in favor of paying promptly any demand made upon the Company, and opposed to obligations or debts accumulating against them, and we find it recorded in two or three instances where Mr. Stoddard moved that a tax of two or more dollars be levied upon each member to pay up deficits. He served his full time and was granted an honorable discharge. For the high standing of the DeWitt Guard to-day, they are in no small degree indebted to Mr. Stoddard. He has enjoyed the confidence of the community sufficient to be elected several times to positions of trust and honor. Long live Samuel Stoddard.

D. L. AVERY, Merchant, enlisted June 24th, 1854. Mr. Avery was a young man of fine attainments, and had every promise of a brilliant future. He manifested much interest in the Company, and although connected with them but a short time, yet sufficiently long to gain the esteem and respect of each member. His death occurred August 24th, 1854. That the loss of Mr. Avery was keenly felt by the Company, the following preamble and resolutions, which were unanimously adopted, will show :

WHEREAS, It has pleased Divine Providence suddenly to take away from our midst by death our much esteemed friend and fellow soldier D. L. Avery, thus depriving us of an active and valued member, and our citizens of one whom but to know was to esteem; and Whereas, The officers and soldiers of the DeWitt Guard feeling and duly appreciating the loss of our universally esteemed member of our corps, and being desirous of giving expression to a spontaneous sentiment of regard for our departed brother in arms, it is therefore unanimously

Resolved, That we do most sincerely mourn the loss of our

late comrade, so suddenly and unexpectedly called away from our ranks by the stern and unrelenting King of Terrors, and that we tender to the partner, brother and sisters of the deceased our heartfelt sympathies in their irreparable loss.

Resolved, That we attend in a body to assist in the last sad duties and ceremonies of the funeral of our late brother, friend and fellow soldier, and that we wear the usual badge of mourning on all parades for thirty days.

Resolved, That the proceedings be signed by our Captain, and a copy thereof be furnished the relatives of the deceased, and also for publication in the village papers.

     P. J. PARTENHEIMER, *Capt, Com'd'g.*
WILLIAM GLENNY, *Sec'y.*

M. E. ELMENDORF, Dentist, enlisted June 30th, 1854. Mr. Elmendorf was a first-class soldier and a tip-top fellow generally. Was particularly celebrated as a fine shot, taking a prize at each of the target shoots while a member. Was an active, energetic young man, and very readily became master of his profession, and is now a Dental Surgeon of considerable note in the city of New York.

LOT S. HINDS, Currier, enlisted July 12th, 1854. Was a good, attentive soldier and a faithful member; served some years with the Company; removed from our village to Danby, where he now resides. Has a son in the United States army.

J. S. PUTNAM, Hotel keeper, enlisted July 12th, 1854. Was a resident but a short time.

IRA M. GARDNER, Mason, enlisted September 18th, 1855. Mr. Gardner served faithfully his seven years, and received an honorable discharge. He has always resided in Ithaca, is a good citizen, a respected man, and a first-class mechanic.

WILLIAM H. HAMMOND, Gas Plumber, enlisted September 23d, 1855. Served his full time and was honorably discharged. Held the office of Company standard-bearer for some years. Was also armory keeper, keeping the guns and equippage in perfect order. We believe the State honestly indebted to him for services rendered, for which he ought to have his pay.

WILLIAM V. BROWN, Currier, enlisted September 26th, 1855. Mr. Brown was celebrated for the great amount of artistic and thoroughly grand music as produced by himself on the base drum. He was Company musician, and remained with them as long as he was a citizen of the place. He is now a resident of Union Springs. "*Big Bill Brown, the Drummer,*" will long be remembered with gratitude by all those connected with the Company during his membership.

K. S. Van Voorhees, Master Mechanic, enlisted July ——, 1854. Colonel VanVoorhees entered the militia service of the State in Feb., 1835, joining the first Company New York Cadets, which was attached as a flank Company to the 2d Regiment N. Y. S. Artillery, (doing duty as Infantry,) and known as the Governor's Guard. In the spring of 1839 he was promoted from Orderly Sergeant, and commissioned as Captain of the Company by Gov. W. H. Seward, he having been unanimously elected to that position by the members of the Company. In the spring of 1840 he was presented with an elegant sword bearing the following inscription:

Presented to
CAPT. K. S. VAN VOORHEES,
By the First Company New York Cadets, as a Token of Esteem and Respect.
New York, April 16th, 1840.

In the Fall of 1840 he visited Ithaca, and having concluded to make this place his permanent residence, he forwarded to New York his resignation in the Spring of 1841. After his removal to this place, he lent his assistance to the drilling and instruction of the Old Ithaca Guard until they were disbanded.

Upon the most urgent solicitations of both officers and men, he consented to become one of the members of the DeWitt Guard. He, possessing probably the greatest amount of military knowledge of any person in the district, was secured by the Company as instructor, and immediately elected Orderly Sergeant. This he did simply as an accommodation, having gained all the military honors he cared to have bestowed upon him before coming to Ithaca.

For us to bestow any compliments upon him in this sketch is perfectly uncalled for, as we produce the following record in place of further remarks:

At the breaking out of the Rebellion he was prevented from entering the service of his country by a severe bodily injury which he had received a few months before; but in the Fall of 1862 he had so far recovered from his lameness, that he ventured to accept the position of Lieutenant Colonel of a Regiment then organizing at Binghamton, N. Y., and afterwards known as the 137th New York Volunteers, to which position he was chosen by the unanimous vote of the War Committee of the 24th Senatorial District.

He immediately entered upon the duty, in connection with Colonel David Ireland, of organizing and disciplining the Regiment, and getting it ready for active service in the field. The want of any knowledge of military tactics by either officers or men, rendered the labor of instructing and drilling the Regiment very arduous, the most of which was performed by Lt. Col. VanVoorhees, Col. Ireland attending to the administrative affairs of the Regiment. Previous to the Regiment's leaving for the seat of war, Lt. Col. VanVoorhees was presented by his friends at Ithaca with a fine horse and set of horse equipments. The Regiment was mustered into the U. S. service on the 25th September, and left for Washington on the 27th, arriving there on the 30th, and were immediately forwarded to Harper's Ferry, Va., by way of Fredericksburgh, Md.; arriving at Harper's Ferry on the 3d October, where they remained until the 10th December, having in the meantime made two important reconnoisances under Gen. Gregg—one to Charlestown and the other to Winchester, Va.

On the 10th December the 12th Army Corps, to which the 137th Regiment had been attached, left Harper's Ferry at the time of Burnside's unsuccessful attack on Fredericksburgh, and having marched to Dumfries, Va., were, in consequence of Burnside's repulse, marched back to Fairfax Station, where they remained until the 17th January, 1863, when they were again ordered forward, Burnside intending to make another attack on Fredericksburgh, but failed on account of the mud.

The 12th Corps having reached Stafford Court House, the Brigade to which the 137th was attached was ordered to Aquia Creek, where they remained until the 26th April, when they commenced their march to Chancellorsville, which they reached on the 29th of April. On the 30th the 12th Corps was ordered forward to feel the enemy's position, and finding them in strong force returned to camp, where they commenced throwing up earthworks, the 137th using bayonets for picks and tin plates for shovels. In the subsequent battles the Regiment maintained its position in the trenches until they were entered by the enemy from the right, (the right flank of the army having been turned by the giving way of the 11th Corps,) when they were ordered to retire, which they did in good order. As this was the first battle in which the Regiment was engaged, some anxiety was felt by the officers as to the mettle of their men; but their conduct on this occasion was such as to give no further uneasiness. After the battle the Regiment returned to Aquia Creek, where it remained until the 13th June, when it commenced its march to Gettysburg, and on the 2d and 3d July was closely and hotly engaged with the invader.

Late in the afternoon of the 2d July the whole of the 12th Corps, with the exception of Green's Brigade, was sent to support the left of the line, which was closely pressed; they had scarcely gone when Stonewall Jackson's old Corps, seven thousand strong, under Ewell, charged our right, which was defended by only Green's Brigade of New York troops less than two thousand strong; but so obstinate was the defence, that the enemy did not succeed in breaking our lines; heavy firing was kept up nearly all night. About four o'clock of the morning of the 3d, the enemy again advanced to the charge but was again repulsed, and a heavy and constant fire was kept up until half past ten, when the enemy retired. The loss of the 137th was four officers and forty-one men killed, and three officers and sixty-four men wounded. Lt. Col. VanVoorhees was slightly wounded twice during the action.

After the battle and the escape of Lee's army across the Potomac, the army again encamped on the banks of the Rappahannock and afterwards on the banks of the Rappidan, when, on the 23d September, immediately after the battle of Chickamauga, the 11th and 12th Corps under Hooker were ordered to Tennessee, where they arrived in the fore part of October. In the latter part of that month Hooker was ordered by Grant to open communication between Bridgport, Ala., and Chattanooga, Tenn., by the way of White Side, along the line of the Memphis and Charleston Railroad. The army of the Cumberland being besieged in Chattanooga and destitute of provisions, it became necessary to secure a shorter line of communication, or the place would have to be abandoned with the loss of all the artillery and trains, as there were no animals left to draw them away. On the 28th of October the 11th Corps under Gen. Howard, followed by a part of Geary's Division of the 12th Corps, all under the command of Gen. Hooker, debouched into Lookout Valley, and for six miles marched in plain view of the rebels who occupied the summit and sides of the mountain, and who could almost count the men in the ranks. On encamping for the night, the 11th Corps was about two and a half miles in advance of Geary's Division, which, being observed by the enemy, they determined to surprise and capture Geary's Division; and accordingly two Divisions of Longstreet's Corps were ordered to the attack. They came in between the 11th Corps and Geary's Division, and while one Division took up a position to prevent reinforcements from being sent to Gen. Geary, the other advanced to the attack, which came near being a surprise, the attack being made about midnight. Gen. Geary had with him at the time but four Regiments and two sections of a battery. The 111th Pennsylvania succeeded in getting into line, and the 137th New York were but partly in line when the enemy opened fire upon them at less than fifty yards distance. These two Regiments bore the whole brunt of the battle, which lasted over two hours; the other two Regiments were placed in position to protect the right flank and rear, leaving the left flank exposed. Early in the action Gen. Green, commanding the Brigade, was wounded, and Col.

Ireland of the 137 Regiment being senior Colonel, the command of the Brigade devolved upon him, leaving the command of the Regiment to Lt. Col. VanVoorhees. The enemy finding the left unprotected, moved a part of their force to the left, and came down on the left and rear of the 137th, but Col. VanVoorhees immediately placed his three left Companies perpendicular to the rear facing them to the left, and facing the rear rank of four other Companies to the rear, the Regiment kept up such a vigorous and well directed fire to the front, flank and rear, as finally to beat back the enemy and cause his retreat, though not till nearly every cartridge in the Regiment was expended.

The 137th (who lost nearly one-third of their number in killed and wounded) was highly complimented for their coolness and courage in this engagement. Gen. Geary in a speech delivered to the Regiment at the time of its muster-out, used the following language in regard to their conduct on this occasion: "I have at all times and in all places given you the credit of saving my Division from rout or capture at Wauhatchie. As I passed down your rear and observed the vigorous attack that was made upon you, I exclaimed, 'My God, if the 137th gives way all is lost.' But thanks to the coolness, skill and courage of your commanding officer, and to your own determined will, you maintained your ground nobly, and the enemy was driven back to his mountain den."

Gen. Howard, in a speech at Philadelphia, characterized this battle as "the wonderful night's revel at Wauhatchie;" and the rebel papers and dispatches acknowledged a serious defeat and heavy loss. Col. VanVoorhees was severely wounded during the action, but refused to leave the field to have his wound dressed until the action was over and all danger of its renewal had passed.

Col. VanVoorhees being at home recovering from his wound, was not with his Regiment in their "battle above the clouds," in which it maintained its reputation, being the first to enter the enemy's works upon Lookout Mountain. Col. VanVoorhees rejoined his Regiment in January, and led it in all the battles of the Atlanta campaign, which commenced on the 2d day of May and ended by the capture of Atlanta on the 2d day of September, being four months of almost continuous fighting. The first battle was that of Mill Creek Gap, May 8th, in which Geary's Division drove the rebels into their works on the summit of Taylor's Ridge. The next was the battle of Resacca, May 15th, in which the Regiment lost several in wounded. The next was the battle of Dallas, or New Hope Church, on the 25th of May; here Hooker's Corps lost heavily. One line of the enemy's works was carried just at night, and they driven about a mile into a second line of works which was not carried owing to the darkness; but a position was taken and a line of works established within a stone's throw of the enemy's line. The Regiment remained here eight days under a constant fire, and without any shelter from the weather. On the 5th June the enemy was found to have evacuated his works, and it was supposed had crossed the Chattahoochie River; the men needing rest the enemy was not followed. The army was moved forward a few miles and put into camp for rest.

On the 7th June, Col. VanVoorhees being officer of the day and having charge of the picket line, discovered the enemy's position; their line extending from Kenesaw Mountain to Lost Mountain, a distance of eight miles. He made a written report of the fact to Gen. Geary, who immediately sent for him and discredited the report, stating that he did not believe there was a rebel soldier this side of the Chattahoochie; he however said he would send up the report. On the 8th June Gen. Sherman telegraphed to the Secretary of War that "his cavalry had that day discovered the enemy's position, and that his right rested on Kenesaw Mountain and his left on Lost Mountain," thus confirming Col. Van-Voorhees' report made the day previous.

On the 15th June the Regiment was moved forward to the foot of Pine Knob, (which was occupied by the enemy,) where they threw up works for the artillery who shelled the hill, one result of which was the killing of Gen. Polk of the rebel army. On the same day the Division moved forward to the attack of Pine Knob; several lines of rifle pits were carried, but the main works were very formidable and were not carried. A line of works were built the same night within a hundred yards of the enemy's line, and heavy skirmishing kept up on the 16th, and on the morning of the 17th the enemy was found to have evacuated his works. The Regiment lost two killed and twenty wounded. The enemy was immediately pursued and found in a new position before noon of the same day. In advancing to support a battery the Regiment lost one man killed and one wounded. On the morning of the 19th the enemy was found to have again abandoned his works, but was found strongly entrenched two miles to the rear. From this time up to the 5th July, when the enemy retreated across the Chattahoochie, it was one continued series of battles, skirmishes, and changes of position.

On the 22d June the 137th Regiment, in connection with the 111th Pennsylvania, were highly complimented by Gen. Hooker for their bravery in obtaining possession of a commanding position which was strongly defended by the enemy.

No forward movement was made from the 7th to the 17th July, the army needing rest and clothing; but on the 17th it again moved forward and crossed the Chattahoochie River. On the 19th the 137th was thrown out as skirmishers, and came upon the enemy's skirmishers at Peach Tree Creek, four miles from Atlanta. The day being excessively warm, and Col. Van-Voorhees' duties as commander of the skirmish line very arduous, he was prostrated by the heat and over exertion, acquiring a disability from which he has not yet fully recovered.

Hooker's Corps crossed Peach Tree Creek on the night of the 19th; and on the 20th. while moving forward to take up a position, were unexpectedly and fiercely attacked by the enemy in a thick piece of woods. Col. VanVoorhees was ordered to move his Regiment by the right flank and take up a position on the right of another Regiment, and in doing so came almost directly upon the enemy's line of battle. Not knowing the position of the rest of the Brigade owing to the thick underbrush, and fearing that if he fell back the right flank of the Brigade would be exposed, he caused his men to maintain their position, which they did manfully for near half an hour, when he learnt that the rest of the Brigade had fallen back some fifteen minutes before, and that his Regiment was left alone battling with the enemy; he immediately gave orders to fall back, when the Regiment retreated from its dangerous position. Loss eight killed and nineteen wounded. Col. VanVoorhees was suffering at the time with a very high fever, and could with difficulty sit on his horse. Many officers in his condition would have got excused and went to the rear, but he never wanted his Regiment to go into action without him ; he became very much attached to it and wished to share all its dangers. On the 22d, being unable to sit up, he was carried to the field hospital ; the Surgeon in charge advised him to make application to be sent to the hospital at Chattanooga ; this he refused to do, saying, that after all the hardships and fighting he had gone through with in the campaign, he did not want to be to the rear when Atlanta was taken. He was, however, on the 25th, against his consent, sent to the hospital at Lookout Mountain. He rejoined his Regiment on the 30th August in time to lead it into Atlanta on the 2d September.

After the death of Col. Ireland, which occurred shortly after entering Atlanta, all the officers present with the Regiment signed a petition to Gov. Seymour, which was handsomely endorsed by the Brigade and Division Commanders, requesting that Lt. Col. VanVoorhees be commissioned as Colonel of the Regiment. Owing to an unjust order from the War Department that " all Regiments reduced below the minimum number should be deprived of its Colonel," he was unable to get mustered, though Gen. Geary made a direct and special request of the Secretary of War, which was endorsed by Gen. Slocum, requesting that he might be mustered into the grade of Colonel as a "reward for his efficiency and gallantry as an officer, his coolness and bravery on the battle-field, and for his general good conduct during the whole of his period of service," but the request was not granted.

The 20th Corps remained in Atlanta until the 15th November, when Gen. Sherman commenced his celebrated "March to the Sea." His march being entirely unopposed, nothing worthy of note occurred until their arrival near Savannah, December 11th. The 137th having been sent out to feel the enemy's position, were deployed as skirmishers, and soon came upon the enemy's skirmishers who were protected by the ruins of some buildings and by a rice field embankment. A lively fire was kept up for some time, when it was deemed advisable to drive them from their position so as to uncover their front. Col. VanVoorhees gave the order to move forward; so impetuous was the charge that the enemy was quickly driven into his works, and could have been driven out and beyond them—as they were seen to leave after firing one round—but as there was no support at hand, Col. VanVoorhees did not deem it prudent to assail the fort, which was defended by several heavy guns, and accordingly recalled his men after several had gained the abattis of the fort, and took up a position behind the rice-field embankment formerly held by the rebel skirmishers, within two hundred yards of the rebel fort.

The Regiment remained here until the 21st December, assisting in the construction of works which could only be done under cover of darkness; the rebel batteries were very active, and the men exposed to a constant shelling; three shells passed through the Quarters of Col. VanVoorhees in one forenoon, and having moved his Quarters to another building, a piece of a shell from a gun-boat passed through his room, taking in its way a table at which he had been sitting but a few minutes previous. The Regiment returned from working on a fort about two o'clock of the morning of the 21st, and shortly after signs of the enemy's evacuating the city were observable, when Capt. S. B. Wheelock of the 137th, with ten men, was sent out to reconnoitre the enemy's works. He found the works abandoned with the guns still standing in position. The fact was reported to the Brigade Commander, who immediately ordered the Brigade forward into the enemy's works, and from thence moved directly into the city, arriving there at daybreak, the 137th was the first to enter the city. The Regiment remained in the city doing guard duty until the 27th January, 1865, when it commenced its march through the Carolinas, arriving at Goldsboro, N. C., on the 24th March.

Col. VanVoorhees having been advised by several of the army Surgeons to seek a change of climate for the recovery of his health, which had been much impaired by exposure and the malarial influence of the climate, he left Savannah January 1st, and was not with his Regiment in their march from Savannah to Goldsboro. He left home February 22d to rejoin his Regiment, but did not succeed in reaching it until its arrival at Goldsboro. On the 10th April Sherman again moved forward in the direction of Raleigh, N. C., which place he reached on the 13th April; here the army remained until the 30th April, when it commenced its march for HOME, arriving at Alexandria, Va., on the 19th

May. The Regiment was mustered out on the 9th June, and ordered to Elmira, N. Y., where it was paid off and discharged on the 18th June, 1865, having been nearly three years in active service.

In giving the military history of Col. Van-Voorhees, we have coupled with his also that of the Regiment, as their histories are one. The officers and men of his command have always spoken well of him; they had confidence in him as a commander, and esteemed him highly as a man. He also enjoyed the confidence and respect of his superior officers, especially of Gen. Geary, who placed the utmost confidence in his ability as an officer, usually appointing him officer of the day when more than usual watchfulness was required, saying that he "always felt safe when Col. VanVoorhees was in command of the picket line. This confidence was also shared in by the Regiment, it being generally selected to occupy the most exposed positions, or lead the column when danger was thought to be imminent.

Col. VanVoorhees was several times (on account of the absence of all its field officers) detailed to command the 149th New York, a Syracuse Regiment of which Gen. Barnum, now State Prison Inspector, was Colonel. On one of these occasions, when about to be relieved and returned to his own Regiment, the following paper was put into his hands, signed by all the officers present with the Regiment:

149TH REG'T N. Y. VOLS.,
Aquia Landing, Va., June 8th, 1863.

COL. K. S. VANVOORHEES:

We, the undersigned, officers of this command, take this opportunity of expressing the feelings of each and every one of us, as the time approaches which must sever the relations that have existed between us and you as our commander. We desire to assure you of our full appreciation of your services, always characterized by kindness and forbearance, and in which the qualities of the gentleman and soldier have commanded our admiration. We desire to thank you for the earnestness and zeal you have exhibited in your endeavors to instruct and better prepare us for the duties devolving upon us, and to assure you that we shall always remember the past four weeks, in which you have been connected with us, with feelings of satisfaction and pleasure; and taking leave of you, as we are about to do, we earnestly hope that in the future *that* success may attend you which industry and fidelity always merit.

At the close of the war Lt. Col. VanVoorhees was appointed Colonel by brevet by the President "for gallant and meritorious services in the late campaigns in Georgia and the Carolinas."

(*Contributed by Capt. B. R. W.*)

JOSEPH ESTY, JR., Clerk, enlisted Sept. 26th, 1855, and was elected Secretary of the Company January 14, 1857. July 28th, 1858, he was first put in the line of promotion by being elected fourth Corporal, and so great was his popularity with the Company, and his knowledge of tactics, that within a trifle over four years from the time of his receiving his chevron as fourth Corporal, he was elected and received his commission as second Lieutenant, (Aug. 25th, 1862,) having filled nearly if not all of the intermediate positions. During the Elmira campaign he was with the Company, steadily refusing to accept of any better fare or accommodations, than the men under his charge received.

While at Barracks No 1, he invariably accompanied his men to the mess house, and prevented many impositions which officers in charge were in the habit of practicing upon soldiers who were obliged to take their rations in that unsavory institution. While the Company were on duty at the rebel prison, no officer did his duty more cheerfully and strictly. He was never known to plead illness to avoid his turn, and the writer of this sketch has, on more than one occasion, known him to take the turn of other officers who plead illness, when he himself was not fit for duty. On one occasion he attended the officer's drill of the Regiment when he was hardly able to leave his tent, and upon the fact being reported to the Colonel, he was peremptorily ordered to his Quarters, to gain the rest which he would not take voluntarily.

No officer in the Regiment stood higher in the estimation of both officers and men, than did Lieut. Esty; and such was the respect of his own Company for him, that upon their return home and the promotion of Captain Blood to the position he now occupies, Lieut. Esty was (Dec. 26th, 1864) elected Captain.

His reluctance to accept the position, showed that he had no aspirations to rise in rank above his fellows, and it was only upon the urgent entreaties of the officers of the Regiment, and his intimate friends, that he was induced to accept the honor thus thrust upon him ; and we venture to say, without any fear of detracting from the worthy merits of his predecessors, that no officer has given more time and money to advance the interest of the Company, than has he—a large proportion of the target prizes for the past two years having been procured by him. At the meeting for target practice August 15th, 1865, Captain Esty was presented by the Company with a splendid sword and belt, which cost about $120. The Captain was taken completely by surprise, as he had received no hint of the matter, and his overcharged feelings prevented him from making known to the Company how highly he prized the gift; but his pleasure at receiving was not greater than the happiness of the donors, in thus having an opportunity of demonstrating their feelings toward him.

The beautiful Armory and Drill-Room now occupied by the Company, are mainly due to his indefatigable efforts.

One prominent feature in the history of the Company, and one which we fear the historian may, from feelings of delicacy, omit, was the splendid supper given, soon after the return of the Company from Elmira, by Captain Esty and lady—an entertainment which was a high testimonial of the Captain's generosity, and the skill and hospitality of Mrs. Esty. The supper will long be remembered by the happy participants.

Captain Esty, in civil life, is no less esteemed than as a soldier, having been for a number of years the confidential clerk and book-keeper in the extensive Leather establishment of Hon. E. S. Esty, an establishment which owes its success in no small degree to his energetic and business qualities.

CHARLES HAUSNER, Carpenter, enlisted October 6th, 1855. Served his full time in the Company. Enlisted Sept. 10th, 1861, in the United States army, in which he served until the 6th day of Sept., 1862, when he was honorably discharged by reason of being totally unserviceable on account of wounds received while in the army. He participated in the battle of Fair Oaks, and received in that one engagement six wounds, while his clothes were pierced by fourteen bullets of the enemy. Probably no soldier ever received the same number of wounds and lived. Upon his return home he was elected Captain of Company E, 50th Regiment National Guard.

A. T. JARVIS, Clerk, enlisted March 19th, 1856. Was a member but a short time.

O. BINGHAM, Boot and Shoe Merchant, enlisted April 2d, 1856. Served his full time, and was honorably discharged from further service in the militia. Upon the breaking out of the

Rebellion he enlisted in Company D, 137th N. Y. Volunteers. August 16th, 1862, was mustered into the United States service at Camp Susquehanna, Binghamton. Soon after the Regiment was ordered to Washington, and from thence to Harper's Ferry, Va., in October, 1862. The Regiment was soon attached to the 12th Army Corps; after a few weeks in camp were ordered to join Gen. Burnside in front of Fredericksburgh, Va. On account of the almost impassibility of the roads, the Regiment did not arrive in time to participate in the fight. Were here ordered into camp at Fairfax, Va., from thence to Aquia Landing, on the Potomac.

The Regiment remained in this camp, perfecting themselves in all the arts of war, until Gen. Hooker had perfected the plan for the battle of Chancellorsville, to which place the Regiment was ordered in the latter part of April, 1863, under command of Gen. Slocum. In this engagement the 137th Regiment did some very hard fighting, and the hero of this sketch came near losing his life while performing acts of kindness to his comrades. He was returning from a spring near by with a number of canteens of water, when he was attacked by a number of rebels who gave him chase through the woods; but our soldier escaped unharmed, although at one time it seemed that nothing short of a miracle could save him. After the battle the Regiment recrossed the Rappahannock and were again in camp.

On the 13th of June Mr. Bingham was promoted to the office of Chief Musician of the Regiment by Col. Ireland for meritorious conduct, and no member of the Regiment or Brigade was more competent to fill this position. This office he held until mustered out of the service.

June 14th the Regiment started for Gettysburg; arrived on the 1st of July and immediately took position on the right of the line. In this battle the Regiment was engaged three days; Chief Musician Bingham had his cap shot off his head as he was carrying a wounded Sergeant from the line; he lost five men of his drum corps, three being wounded and two captured.

In September the 11th and 12th Corps were detached from the army of the Potomac and ordered to Tennessee. The men were transported in cattle cars, and reached the city of Nashville after about ten days travel; from thence were moved to Wauhatchie Valley. In this valley one Brigade, composed of the 137th and other Regiments, in all about one thousand men, were attacked by the rebel General Hood with four thousand picked men; the enemy finally withdrew to Lookout Mountain. In this fight our Chief Musician had his bugle, which was hanging by his side, pierced with a bullet and destroyed.

After several other engagements in this vicinity, the enemy were routed, and the men ordered to prepare for the taking of Atlanta, which city was captured by the Union forces Sept. 2d, 1864, Chief Musician Bingham marching in command of the drum corps of his Division playing the familiar tune Yankee Doodle, to the disgust of the inhabitants of that city.

From this time comparative quiet reigned until November 14th, when commenced the great "March for the Sea Coast," which was so successfully accomplished, as also the march from Savannah to Richmond, from which point the army were moved by easy marches to Washington, at which city they were mustered out of the service as fast as possible. Our Chief Musician was mustered out near Washington June 9th, 1865, and immediately sent with the Regiment to Elmira, where they were paid and honorably discharged June 20th.

He was in the service nearly three years; never lost a day's duty from his Regiment; he participated in every engagement of the Regiment from the time it entered the field, and fully proved himself to be a soldier of ability and courage, possessing all the qualities that are requisite to make a first-class American soldier.

Now that he has returned to his home and friends, we all unite in bestowing upon him the honor he so dearly bought, and respect and cherish him as one of the defenders of our common country.

H. W. BISHOP, Druggist, elected May 31st, 1856. Doctor Bishop was an excellent member; served the Company as Treasurer for two years; filled most of the non-commissioned offices, and was esteemed highly by all the members, as he was by the community at large. He was Orderly Sergeant at the time he left the Company and joined the United States army. Very soon after his enlistment in the service of his country, he was promoted to hospital Steward, which position he filled until removed by death. Many there are, besides his near relatives and the

Company of which he was a member, who mourn the loss of Doctor Bishop.

E. S. CONKLIN, enlisted June 9th, 1856. The writer is wholly unacquainted with the history of this member.

E. B. TORREY, Banker, enlisted September 10th, 1856. No member ever connected himself with the DeWitt Guard who took more interest in the Company than did Mr. Torrey; and although his profession was such that it would seem impossible for him to spend any very great amount of time with the Company, still through the kindness and leniency of President J. B. Williams, and Cashier, Colonel Hardy, he almost always answered to his name at all the drills and parades of the Company. At the business meeting he was particularly useful, always lending his advice, and eager to do any thing that would increase the interest of the members. Always scrupulously prompt in meeting his obligations, and we believe during the several years of his membership, he never allowed his dues to run over one month; he filled most of the non-commissioned offices; as a soldier he liked every other soldier, and every other soldier liked him; and the only way he could ever

dissolve his membership, was by the expiration
of his term of enlistment. He most creditably
served his time and received an honorable discharge. He retired from the Bank a short time
since, and secured a patent for "Torrey's Patent
Artesian Wells," which is a most valuable invention, and is being universally used wherever introduced. We extend to him our hearty congratulations for the success he has already attained, and earnestly hope that our friend will
realize his full anticipations in his new enterprise.

M. R. BARNARD, Principal of Public School,
enlisted Sept. 10th, 1856. Mr. Barnard served
his full time and was honorably discharged from
further service in the militia. He served the
Company as Secretary for a year or more. He
is still represented by his son, Corporal E. E.
Barnard; is brother of John Barnard, the hero
of Lookout Mountain. Has been for many years
Principal of our Public School, having some
times as many as eight hundred scholars. In
this situation, as well as every other one, he
gave the most perfect satisfaction, and the regrets were many that we heard expressed when
he determined to withdraw from the school, and

still many more when it became known that he had fully determined to change his residence to Louisville, Ky.

Prof. Barnard is a thorough scholar, a man of great and comprehensive mind, fine intellect, and a man in every way qualified to hold the very first position in society wherever he may go. When in his new home he becomes as well known as he is here, we know he will be equally respected. Success and prosperity ever attend him.

Marcus Lyon, Lawyer and District Attorney, elected January 20th, 1857. Mr. Lyon soon discovered that it would require more of his time than he could possibly devote to this purpose, and furnished a substitute in the person of the lamented Wager.

Luther Losey, Harness-Maker, enlisted June 27th, 1857. Mr. Losey served his time, was a good soldier and a fine mechanic, else he could not have found employment so many years in the establishment of Colonel Millspaugh. He is now a resident of one of the Western States.

Henry S. Krum, Shoe Merchant, enlisted May 18th, 1858. Mr. Krum served but a very short time as a member of this Company, but sufficiently long to prepare him to assume command of a Company upon his entering the United States service. He was in the service for some time, and upon his return home was elected Captain of the Caroline Company, National Guard, which position he still holds.

JOHN C. HAZEN, Merchant, enlisted May 18th, 1858. We have very frequently, through this History, mentioned instances where the Company were indebted to individual members for some particular acts, or the interest they have manifested in the general good and prosperity of the Company. In this instance, however, we have the contrary. We believe Lieut. Hazen is more indebted to the DeWitt Guard, than any person now living, and on this point we are sure we shall satisfy the reader.

July 12th, 1857, the Company visited the city of Auburn, (an account of which will be found in the History of the Company). While there, they were several times the guests of a number of distinguished citizens of that city. At a very elaborate and magnificent entertainment given in honor of the Company, by Hon. B. F. Hall, the subject of this sketch formed the acquaintance of the daughter of our host. Auburn's fairest daughters were there. The elite of the city were represented. Among them all, the choice of our friend was the lady just mentioned. The result of the acquaintance that evening formed, is generally known. Little did the good people of Auburn think that our excursion was to be the means of depriving them of one of their fairest daughters. Auburn, the loveliest city of the plain, the loser; but Ithaca, the Forest City, the gainer. All must concede that no one was more deserving, or better entitled to the prize, than our respected soldier. A very noticeable and singular incident in connection with our excursion to Auburn, we came near forgetting, which should be mentioned here. It is this: that at that time, Sergeant Hazen was Company Secretary, and the account of that trip, so fully and graphically given, in another part of this book, is taken verbatim from his minutes.

As we have noticed, Mr. Hazen enlisted in May, 1858. He was permitted to remain but a short time in the ranks, but filled all of the non-commissioned offices, and was Orderly Sergeant while in the United States service, which is a position of much importance, and also one where the utmost caution must be used, or the occupant will soon find that his comrades are exceedingly dissatisfied with him; it being the duty of the Orderly to make the various details. But in this instance, there was never one word of complaint. The Orderly, in his pleasant manner, would say to the men: "Please report for duty, to-morrow morning," and invariably the men were there. Every member of the Company, not only but very many officers and men with whom we were associated while in Elmira, became very much attached to Sergeant Hazen; and all this, not without cause, for certainly he was one of the very best men in camp. To show that he was appreciated, very soon after the Company returned from Elmira, they elected him First Lieutenant, which commission he now holds.

Lieutenant Hazen is not only a fine soldier, and a good and respected officer, but as a citizen and a business man, he has very few superiors. The firm of Stowell & Hazen is known throughout the county, and they enjoy the confidence of as large a class of customers, as any House in Western New York. They conform to a strict degree of honesty in small as well as large transactions, and by this means have built up a reputation second to none in the State.

EDWARD D. NORTON, Printer, enlisted June 17, 1858. His qualifications as a soldier, were sufficiently good to entitle him to fill the posts of Corporal and Sergeant in a worthy and creditable manner. He was employed for many years in the *Ithaca Journal* office, but finally removed to the city of Rochester, where he now resides.

WILLIAM BYINGTON, Merchant, enlisted June 21st, 1858. Mr. Byington served his full time, and was honorably discharged. He was a good soldier, an equally good Corporal, and a better Sergeant. At the time the Company were called into the United States service, it was impossible for Sergeant Byington to accompany them; Lieut. Kenney, his partner, being an officer in the Company, it was desirable to have him, and of course both could not leave; but the Sergeant, at considerable expense, furnished a satisfactory substitute. He was never behind his comrades in contributing in any way that would be for the general good of the institution. He is one of the enterprising merchants of this place, and all acquainted with him can testify to his equally good qualifications as a citizen, that we have as a soldier.

WILLIAM L. MINTURN, Mason, enlisted June 17th, 1858. Was a faithful and attentive soldier, served his full time and received an honorable discharge. There is no better man in the community than Mr. Minturn. As for his reputation as a Master Mechanic, we refer the reader to the many buildings erected under his supervision in our village.

SILAS R. ZIMMER, Clerk, enlisted July, 20th, 1858. Mr. Zimmer served a number of years with the Company to the most perfect satisfaction of both officers and men. He was one of the employees of that prince of merchants, L. H. Culver, Esq.

A. BRUM, Clothing Merchant, enlisted July 27th, 1858. Was connected with the Company but a short time. Removed, we believe, to the city of New York.

PHILIP S. RYDER, Artist, enlisted July 27th, 1858. Mr. Ryder performed well the duties of a member of this Company so long as he remained a resident of the district. We believe he is now a resident of Cleveland, O.

LEVI KENNEY, Merchant, enlisted June 24th,

1858. After serving a very short time as private, was elected Corporal, promoted to Sergeant, and finally to first Lieutenant, which commission he held until the expiration of his term of enlistment, when he resigned. Lieutenant Kenney was a stirring and an energetic officer. The command of the Company devolved upon him much of the time while in the United States army, and at one time was in command of the Regiment. The Company had been but a few days at Elmira, when Lieut. Kenney was selected from among all the officers to command a very large detachment of substitutes, drafted men and bounty-jumpers to the Head-Quarters of Gen. Grant's army. He selected his officers and Guard with care, and we think his report upon his return, to the Commander of the Post, was as satisfactory as any return ever made to him. This is the only instance that occurred while there, of the command being given to an officer of less rank than Captain. The Lieutenant was detailed from his command on three different occasions and commissioned one of the court-martial for the trial of officers only. He was elected clerk of the court, and the records were kept by him equally well as by one who had long been familiar with the duties of an office of that kind. He was one of the best officers in the Regiment, thoroughly familiar with his duties, and required of his men (as do all good officers) a prompt and willing obedience to all commands. He was complimented on several occasions by Col. Wisner, commanding the Regiment; also received honorable mention by Major Beal, of the veteran Reserve Corps, and by Col. Moore, commanding the Post.

Soon after returning from Elmira his term of service expired, and he resigned his commission and was granted an honorable discharge. No officer or enlisted man ever served his term with more fidelity than did Lieut. Kenney, and no officer was more entitled to the respect of his men. He is the senior partner in the firm of Kenney, Byington & Co., the only exclusively Dry-Goods House in Ithaca; and their splendidly arranged and well filled store, together with the vast amount of patronage they enjoy, is sufficient proof that he is as well appreciated as a citizen and business man, as he was a soldier and officer.

JAMES H. SMITH, Tin-Smith, enlisted September 2d, 1858. As long as Mr. Smith was a citizen of Ithaca he was a member in good standing in this Company. Our recollection is that he served about three years. He removed to Elmira.

P. B. WAGER, Lawyer, enlisted January 5th, 1859. Remained with the Company until he enlisted in the service of his country. No young man ever started in life with a more brilliant prospect than did Mr. Wager; had but a short time previous to his enlistment in the United States army been admitted to the bar, and had commenced the practice of Law with very marked success. At the outbreak of the Rebellion he enlisted in Company I, 32d New York Volunteers, and received a Lieutenancy, which commission he held until the time of his death. He died in camp, and his remains were forwarded to his home and buried with military honors by this Company, assisted by the entire Fire Department of the village. Lieutenant Wager was a patriotic soldier and a courageous officer.

D. A. McKAY, Cigar Manufacturer, enlisted May 12th, 1859. Served as a member of this Company until his enlistment in the United States army. Was soon commissioned Lieutenant, and faithfully served until the close of the war. We have been unable to collect as full a history of Lieutenant McKay as we would have been glad to have given; but we are able to say, however, that his war history was an honorable one, and he has a lasting claim upon his fellow citizens for gallant services rendered his country during the hour of her peril.

C. C. GREENLY, Merchant, enlisted September 27th, 1859. But a very short period of time elapsed between his enlistment and the time when he was duly confirmed fourth Corporal of Company A. Step by step he advanced until commissioned a Lieutenant by Gov. Fenton, which commission he now holds. Each office he has filled most honorably, and no member stands higher in the estimation of the Company to-day than Lieut. Greenly. While serving in the army, he performed the duties that devolved upon him in a manner that would have been highly creditable to an officer of many years experience.

It was the pleasure of the writer to be associated with Lieut. Greenly and others who were in charge of a detail of men whose destination was the Head-Quarters of Gen. Grant at City Point, and too much credit cannot be awarded the Lieutenant for the care with which he guarded his men, turning over to the authorities at City Point every man of his command, while others would be short five or six, and sometimes many more; all in his charge were either drafted men, substitutes, or deserters. The writer most thoroughly appreciated the company of Lieut. Greenly in that expedition, and wishes to acknowledge many favors shown him.

It may be supposed by many that the duties of the members of the DeWitt Guard at Elmira were not very arduous; but in this particular instance we know the contrary to be the case. Aside from the regular camp duties, (which a portion of the time were very severe,) the Lieutenant carried on an extensive correspondence, the satisfactory termination of which resulted in the marriage of our respected officer soon after his return from the field.

W. F. FINCH, Merchant, enlisted May 1st, 1860. During nearly six years of membership, we find Mr. Finch marked absent from the drills but three or four times—surely a good introduction. Not only in attendance, however, was he regular and punctual, but in every other duty required of him as a member of the Company. So particular was he not to be in arrears on the Company's books, that we believe there was not six months of his membership that the Company were not indebted to him for dues and taxes paid in advance. He enjoyed the exercise of the drill, and became perfectly familiar with the tactics and evolutions; took great pride in being a good soldier. Against his wishes he was elected Corporal, and by various promotions reached the position of second Sergeant. A little more than a year ago we were deprived of the pleasure of the further direct membership of our respected Sergeant, by the interposition of our esteemed Colonel, H. D. Barto, who, discovering in him a man with the qualifications of a perfect soldier, appointed him to a position on his staff, which, after due consideration, he accepted. Still he retains his membership in the Company so far as paying his dues are concerned. He is a member of the firm of Morrison, Hawkins & Finch, the leading Dry-Goods House of the place.

EDGAR M. FINCH, Book-Keeper, enlisted June 6th, 1860. Is brother of Sergeant W. F. Finch, and the same must be said in his case, so far as holding office is concerned, with one exception. He has filled every non-commissioned office

—is now Orderly Sergeant. He served with his Company during their term of enlistment in the United States army. No better soldier can be found, not even in the regular army, than Sergeant Finch. The most regular attendant at the drills, meetings and parades, of any member ever connected with the Company. As will be noticed, he enlisted over six years ago, and during that time has never paid a fine. He is one of the most unassuming, yet one of the noblest and most generous young men of Ithaca.

JOHN C. HEATH, Wholesale and Retail Grocer, enlisted September 4th, 1860.

We know of no one who has devoted more time, or distributed more money to build up, keep in existence and sustain the military organizations of the day, than Quartermaster Heath. Whatever he becomes interested in, either in a military or business way, he invariably drives to a successful termination. In the organization of the Regiment he took an active part, and we know Colonel Barto must feel under great indebtedness to him for rendering invaluable assistance in organizing and mustering in the service many of the new Companies.

While connected with the Company he was

one of its best members and warmest supporters; and although at the present time in no way directly connected with them as a Company, he still manifests a deep interest in its prosperity. His first office was fourth Corporal, from which he was promoted to Quartermaster Sergeant upon the non-commissioned staff of Col. H. A. Dowe, (since promoted to Brigadier General.) Upon the reorganization of the Regiment, he accepted the commission of Quartermaster upon the staff of Colonel Barto, which he now holds, the duties of which for the past year and a half have been onerous, having distributed to the various Companies of the Regiment all their arms, clothing and other equipage, besides performing other duties not directly in the line of his office. The officers, as well as the men of the 50th Regiment, owe Quartermaster Heath a debt of gratitude, which we are led to believe will only be cancelled by their continuing to sustain and keep alive the interest they have recently manifested in their Companies, and make the Regiment one of the best in the State.

We congratulate our friend on being associated in business with James B. Taylor, Esq., the most celebrated of all Ithaca Grocery merchants. The firm of J. B. Taylor & Co. is known from New York to Chicago, and from Boston to New Orleans, as the most responsible and most accommodating of any establishment of the kind between these extreme points ; also, for keeping the largest stock of goods, and selling them the cheapest, of any House outside of the great cities.

With Quartermaster Heath to look after the interest of the militia, and Alderman Taylor that of his constituents and the general welfare of our village, we may consider ourselves safe beyond the possibility of a doubt.

H. W. JACKSON, JR., Merchant, enlisted September 4th, 1860. Very soon after joining this Company he enlisted in the United States service, being one of the organizers of Company I, 32d New York Volunteers. Was elected first Lieutenant, which commission he held for about a year and a half, when his health failing he was compelled to resign. He was engaged in two or three battles under Gen. Franklin.

C. WOODWORTH, Merchant, enlisted September 4th, 1860. Mr. Woodworth was most an estimable man in every respect. During the short time he was connected with the Company, every member became warmly and firmly attached to him.

He removed from this place to Fon Du Lac, Wis., where he had been a resident but a short time when, in the all-wise Providence of God, he was called to that Heavenly City for which he, in a most eminent degree, was prepared to enter.

GEORGE H. GRANT, Clerk, enlisted April 23d, 1861. Served faithfully as a member of this Company, also in the United States army and in the United States navy. Was most thoroughly appreciated by the members of this Company. During the Elmira campaign he was one of the great alleviators of that terrible disease—homesickness. Will long be remembered as one of the celebrated Quartette—Grant, Wilson, Betts and Johnson.

E. J. FARNHAM, Clerk, enlisted April 23d, 1861. Was one of the first soldiers that enlisted from this place in the United States army. Served honorably in Company A, 32d New York Volunteers, until in consequence of disease contracted in the army, he was no longer qualified to serve and was honorably discharged. Was a good soldier, and sacrificed his health for the honor of his country.

ADNAH NEYHART, Speculator, enlisted April 23d, 1861. By reason of his profession, Mr. Neyhart was much of the time separated from the Company, but always prompt in meeting his obligations and sustaining the Company in every possible way, aside from being personally present. Furnished a substitute who represented him in the United States army, suffered many reverses in business, but fortunately his last investment was a good one—*he struck oil*—and is now again "*sound.*"

We congratulate him; no one has worked harder for, or is better entitled to, a two hundred and fifty barrel well than Adnah.

THOMAS A. BROWN, Tin-Smith, enlisted April 23d, 1861. Was an active member during the short time he was a resident of the village.

R. W. HEGGIE, Clerk, enlisted July 3d, 1861. No young man ever joined this Company that evinced more interest in its success and general welfare, than did Mr. Heggie, and no member was more respected. He was in every way calculated to win the esteem and friendship of all with whom he became associated. He very readily became a perfect soldier. With a fervent love for his country, and a desire to do something for its defence in the hour of its peril, he enlisted, August 26th, 1863, in Company G, 15th New York Cavalry; was soon elected first Sergeant, and May 24th, 1864, was commissioned Lieutenant. Was engaged in many battles, in one of which he was wounded and a short time separated from his Company. He was a courageous officer, always ready to dash into the conflict. Several times he was in command of troops, conveying them from Boston to Charleston; was then entrusted by Government with a position of great responsibility and importance, but at all times was equal to his duties. He faithfully served until the close of the war, and was honorably mustered out. Is now connected with one of the largest cotton establishments of the South, and located at Galveston, Texas.

JOHN S. GAY, Clerk, enlisted July 3d, 1861. Was a member until July 7th, 1865; was with the Company during their term of service in the army; a good soldier that could be trusted, and he accompanied several detachments to the front. Is now engaged in business at Cairo, Ill.

W. H. KELLOGG, Tobacconist, enlisted July 3d, 1861. Served as a member until July 7th, 1865. Volunteered in the United States army

Sept. 2d, 1864, and honorably served the full term of his enlistment.

HENRY A. ST. JOHN, Merchant, enlisted July 3d, 1861. Although his name is recorded as enlisting July 3d, 1861, he had, however, been connected with the Company a long time previous to that date, but in a capacity that would not admit of his signing the roll and becoming a regular member under the statute. Displaying a taste for the science of military while a mere boy, he was elected by the members of this Company one of their markers. At the time he became a full member he was well versed in the school of the soldier, and familiar with the school of the Company. Was soon elected fourth Corporal, being the youngest member that had ever held office; was gradually promoted until he reached the post of second Sergeant, which position he now fills. Sergeant St. John particularly distinguished himself while at Elmira; was one of the best non-commissioned officers of the Regiment. Col. R. P. Wisner, commanding the 58th Regiment, twice appointed him to fill vacancies occasioned by absence of officers of his staff. Was the first Sergeant detached from the Regiment and placed in charge over substitutes and deserters, en route for City Point, arriving at his destination without the loss of a man. He fully understood his duty, enforcing strict discipline, and requiring his men to conform to all the regulations and articles of war, but equally careful not to exceed the bounds of his authority.

He is one of the most active men of the Company; always first in any enterprise, the object of which is the good of the organization. He has contributed much toward this History by giving a detailed and very accurate account of the Elmira campaign, which may be found on another page. It is a pleasure to be associated with him as a soldier, or socially in the ordinary walks of life. Is a member of the firm of G. W. Baker & Co., the popular Dry-Goods House of the place.

M. L. GRANGER, Merchant, enlisted July 3d, 1861. In time and money Mr. Granger has sacrificed much for the sake of being a soldier. Always present at parades, drills or meetings, and always prompt to meet his obligations. He volunteered in the United States service with the Company in 1864, shared the pleasures and deprivations of camp life with his comrades. For the fatherly care and attention shown the younger members, and those who needed assistance in any way, he was named and known in camp by the title of " Uncle Amos." He honestly served out the term of his enlistment and was honorably discharged. Is partner in the firm of J. S. Granger & Co., a very extensive Dry-Goods House, who enjoy the reputation of keeping the most carefully selected stock of goods of any establishment of the kind in Central New York.

ROBERT GOODWIN, Baker, enlisted July 3d, 1861. A good soldier and an upright man. Was employed in the Bakery department of the extensive establishment of John L. Whiton, Esq. Removed West about three years ago.

JAMES STANYON, Blacksmith, enlisted July 3d, 1861. Was Company musician, and served as such until he volunteered in the United States service. He was a worthy and honorable soldier, engaged in many battles. We have been unable to obtain his war history for publication.

HENRY W. COLLINS, Clerk, enlisted July 3d, 1861. Like Sergeant St. John, Mr. Collins was one of the Company markers long before he became a regular member. Was a soldier of merit, and liked by all the members. Served the

Company as Secretary ; his skillful penmanship, as shown upon the records, would be of itself a sufficient recommendation ; but "*none need apply,*" as he is now first book-keeper in the New York office of Adams' Express Company. His absence is temporary, however, as he still considers Ithaca his residence, and is still a member of this Company.

JOHN C. GAUNTLETT, Druggist, enlisted September 4th, 1861. Mr. Gauntlett has always been as popular as a soldier, as he is a citizen and associate. He is of the class that we would always like to retain as members ; but to meet the demands of superior officers, we are obliged to relinquish our claim upon them. Starting from the ranks, Sergeant Gauntlett had reached the post of fourth Sergeant, when Colonel Barto selected him as Regimental Standard-bearer, which office he now holds. Not feeling disposed to leave his old friends, however, he retains his membership and position in the Company, and still acts with them, except on Regimental parade. He volunteered with the Company in the United States service, and well and faithfully served out the term of his enlistment.

He is engaged in the Drug and Medicine business, and it is a matter of pride to him, and a source of gratification to his numerous friends, that he stands at the head of that branch of trade in Tompkins county.

IRVING W. NORTON, Cigar-Maker, enlisted September 4th, 1861. Was a good soldier while connected with the Company. Volunteered in the United States service, and received a bayonet wound near his right eye. By this he was prevented from being with his Company for a short time, when he again resumed his duties and served the full term of his enlistment. Mr. Norton, and the night he was wounded, will long be remembered by the DeWitt Guard.

JOHN L. MANDEVILLE, Civil Engineer and Surveyor, enlisted October 2d, 1861. A prompt and systematic soldier, and a most excellent member of the Company. Although a resident of the town of Caroline, is as frequently at the drills as many who live in town. Has always taken a great interest in the Company, accompanied them to Elmira, and volunteered in the United States service. Was permitted to serve but a short time with the Company, however, as he was detailed chief Clerk at Colonel Moore's Head-Quarters; he was, nevertheless, always ready for any kind of duty, when not engaged in his office. While acting as sentinel (relieving one of the guard for a play spell) one night, he alone arrested two desperate characters, who were stealing from the camp of the 58th Regiment, for which he received a unanimous vote of thanks. He served the full term of his enlistment, and was honorably discharged, since which time, until recently, he has been engaged in civil engineering in and around Washington and Baltimore. He has now returned, and can be addressed at Mott's Corners, Tompkins county, N. Y.

E. K. JOHNSON, Clerk, enlisted March 10th, 1862. Mr. Johnson, better known as "Kirk," was honored with a non-commissioned office. Served with the Company as Secretary, and from his records we make extracts elsewhere. Was a capital soldier, a perfect gentleman, and a first rate fellow generally. Volunteered and served in the United States service with the DeWitt Guard at Elmira. No more daring soldier ever stood up before a live Johnny, than he; was detailed as police—the celebrated quartette, Johnson, Betts, Grant and Wilson—and we can assure the reader that every thing within their reach was perfectly safe. Consistent with their obligations as police officers, they watched the various hen-roosts, and other places likely to be disturbed by unruly soldiers; and not more than fifteen or sixteen times did they find in the cook stove oven of Company A, turkeys, chickens, ducks, and other domestic fowls. At the close of his term of service in the army, he made an engagement with a large establishment at the West, where he has since resided. He has warm and *peculiar* attachments to the place of his birth, and we earnestly hope it may yet be his permanent residence.

A. H. PLATTS, Grocer, enlisted March 7th, 1862. Retained his membership but a very short time.

W. H. HOSFORD, Mechanic, enlisted August 6th, 1862. Served honorably in the United States army. We should have been glad to have published his war history, but have been unable to procure it.

JAMES H. BISHOP, Carpenter, enlisted August 6th, 1862. August 16th, 1862, Mr. Bishop volunteered in the United States army for three years, unless sooner discharged. Soon after enlisting, he joined Captain John H. Terry's Company, which was connected with the 137th Regiment, commanded by Col. David Ireland, and subsequently by Col. K. S. VanVoorhees. Before leaving Binghamton was elected Corporal. The first camp duty performed by Corporal Bishop, was picket duty on Bolivar Heights; the weather becoming severely cold, and he being placed upon the "lookout," which was the highest point on the Heights, he suffered more from cold and exposure than he did during all the time he was in the service. This post he occupied one week; soon after this the camp was removed to Fairfax Station. April 27th was ordered to pack and be ready to move. The baggage of each soldier consisted of his clothes, tent, blankets, eight day's rations, and one hundred and sixty rounds of cartridges, with gun and accroutrements. Corporal Bishop was engaged in each day's battle at Chancellorsville, which were the 1st, 2d and 3d days of May. Was next engaged at the battle of Gettysburg, where he was constantly fighting for three days. After the return of the Regiment to Virginia, Corporal Bishop was detailed for special duty, and sent to Elmira on recruiting service, at which place he remained until April, 1864, when he again joined his regiment at Stevenson, Ala. Was engaged in the skirmishes around Resacca, and finally in the battle at that place, which was from the 12th to the 15th of May. Participated in the sharp fight at Dallas Woods, also at Pine Knob and the severe battle of Peach Tree Creek. After these and many other battles of less account, the Regiment marched into the city of Atlanta at midnight, the band playing "The Campbells are Coming." Thus ended a campaign of four months.

Again taking up a line of march toward Milledgeville, the only obstructions they met were the railroads, which were speedily rendered useless by taking up the track, heating the rails in a fire made of the ties, and then twisting them around the nearest tree or stump. Being obliged to depend upon the country through which they passed for subsistence, foraging parties were each day sent out, and supplies of sweet potatoes, pork and poultry would be brought in by them, upon which they lived like nabobs. After marching many days and much skirmishing, they finally entered the city of Savannah about sunrise on the morning of the 22d day of December. From this time up to the time of the muster-out of the Regiment, Corporal Bishop was every day ready for duty, losing no time by sickness or otherwise. Was finally mustered out with his Regiment and honorably discharged. All honor to Corporal James H. Bishop of the 137th Regiment New York Volunteers.

He is now settled down again in his old home, receiving the congratulations of his friends, and prepared at all times to assist them " to a new house," or accommodate them in any way in the line of his profession.

A. L. BISHOP, Carpenter, enlisted August 6th, 1862. Soon after joining the DeWitt Guard, Mr. Bishop volunteered in the United States service, into which he was mustered Aug. 16th, 1862, in Captain J. H. Terry's Company, 137th New York Volunteers. Before leaving Binghamton, the first place of rendezvous of the Regiment, Mr. Bishop was elected and appointed first Duty Sergeant of the Regiment. He left Binghamton with his Regiment for the seat of war Sept. 27th, 1862. The first camp of any account was at Pleasant Valley, where our Sergeant experienced rather hard fare—being obliged to eat rations which would, by very fastidious persons, have been considered rather unpalatable—but of course soldiers must get used to most every thing, and so our friend made the best of his "hard tack" and *fresh meat*. On the 10th day of December he was elected and appointed Orderly Sergeant, filling the vacancy occasioned by the death of Orderly Sergeant M. L. Beers. Arrived at Aquia Jan. 27th, 1863. The duty here was very severe, consisting of camp guard, picket guard, ordinance guard, railroad guard and fatigue duty. Remained in camp at this point until the last of April, when orders were received to be ready to march at a moment's warning, which orders were carried into execution April 27th, when the Rappahannock was crossed at Kelly's Ford, moving in the direction of Chancellorsville, where the Company were engaged the 1st, 2d and 3d days of May, on each of which Sergeant Bishop took an active part.

On the 8th day of June he was commissioned and mustered as second Lieutenant of Company D, vice Lieutenant Whitmore resigned. Was engaged the 2d and 3d days of July in the battle of Gettysburg. Was in command of troops that guarded the wagon trains from Nashville, Tenn., to Bridgeport, Ala. Also marched and guarded a wagon train to Chattanooga; arriving as far as Wauhatchie halted for the night, comfortably rolling themselves in their blankets preparatory to a good night's rest. About eleven o'clock firing was heard upon the picket line, when they were ordered out and soon in line, which had hardly been done before they received a sharp volley of musketry from the rebels. The fight lasted until three o'clock of the next morning. The killed, wounded and missing of the 137th Regiment in this engagement was ninety men. Lieut. Bishop also participated in the famous fight at Lookout Mountain, and that of Ringold, Ga.

May 2d, 1864, he commenced the great Georgia campaign with Gen. Sherman; was engaged in the battle of Resacca from the 12th to the 15th of May, and on the 25th in the battle of Dallas Wood; the next engagement was at Pine Knob on the 15th of June; had continued skirmishing until the 20th of July, when occurred the battle of Peach Tree Creek, Ga., after which they rested until the 23d, when they moved in front of Atlanta; marched into the city Sept. 2d at twelve o'clock, after a campaign of over four months.

October 24th Lieut. Bishop was commissioned and mustered first Lieutenant of Company D, vice Lieut. C. C. Kellogg resigned. October 25th he was sent out with a foraging party; were out four days and returned with five hundred wagon loads of forage. November 1st started for home on a twenty days leave of absence, and eight of the days were occupied in getting there; upon his return he found the Regiment at Savannah. January 27th he was ordered to the hospital, being wholly unfit for duty; was detained there twenty days; was again with the Regiment at Raleigh, N. C., where orders were received to be ready forthwith to march for Richmond, the Confederacy having succumbed to the government of the United States. Passed through Richmond the 11th of May, crossed the Rappahannock at U. S. ford the 15th, and arrived at Alexandria on the 19th. May 23d he received an order stating that he was honorably discharged from further service by reason of physical disability; arrived at his home in Ithaca June 20th, 1865.

No more worthy soldier or respected officer ever enlisted or commanded a Company, than Lieut. A. L. Bishop; and a more honorable record than his cannot be produced—always ready to do his whole duty to his comrades and his country.

J. H. TERRY, Lawyer, enlisted August 4th, 1862. Had belonged to the Company but a short time when he enlisted in the United States service, and was elected Captain of a Company organized in this village. We have been unable to obtain his war history. He is now engaged in his profession at the West.

B. R. WILLIAMS, Junior Editor of the Ithaca Citizen and Democrat, enlisted September 3d, 1862. Captain Williams, while connected with the Company, was one of its most useful members, and it gives us pleasure to be afforded this opportunity to acknowledge our obligations, and also to accord to him the honor which is his due.

He was permitted to remain as a private in the Company but a very short time before he was elected Corporal, and by promotion reached the position of Sergeant, in which capacity he enlisted in the United States service with this Company in September, 1864; there, after a short time, the Company were deprived of his services by reason of his accepting a position upon the staff of Col. R. P. Wisner, which, however, did not separate him from his former associates. Captain Williams, by his many acts of personal kindness toward the members of the DeWitt Guard while in the service, and particularly toward the officers, in rendering them the most invaluable assistance in arranging and closing up their account, was entitled to and received their most hearty thanks. He rendered very many acts of kindness officially which were in no way connected with the duties of his office, but it seemed to be a pleasure for him to do any thing for the officers and men of his former Company. He was constantly on terms of the most perfect friendship with the officers and men of the Regiment, and was a particular favorite with all.

While a member of the Company he filled the office of Secretary, and we are permitted to copy extracts from his minutes which we do on another page. Very soon after returning from Elmira, he was commissioned Captain of Engineers in the 50th Regiment, National Guard. Notwithstanding his promotion, he still insists upon retaining his membership in the DeWitt Guard, against which not one objection is known to exist; it is the strong desire of every member of the Company that he may continue such, as long as they are in any way connected with said institution.

M. L. THOMPSON, Speculator, enlisted September 8th, 1862. Removed from the District soon after enlisting ; sought his fortune in the oil wells of Pennsylvania, which adventures, we are pleased to state, have been successful.

GEORGE E. HALSEY, Druggist, enlisted September 23d, 1862. Served with the Company until he represented himself in the United States army by substitution, when he withdrew from this Company. Is proprietor of the celebrated Fountain Drug Store of this village.

VERNON J. TERRY, Tobacconist, enlisted September 23d, 1862. Mr. Terry is the third member of the same family who have served as members of this Company. On account of business it was impossible for him to personally accompany his comrades during their service in the United States army,—but generously furnished a substitute at an expense to him of over one hundred dollars. He is one of the large tobacco and cigar manufactures of this village, and his brand upon the weed is a sure indication of prime stock.

ALFRED BROOKS, Hat, Cap and Fur Merchant,

enlisted October 1st, 1862. Is now fourth Sergeant of the Company; is a favorite, not only of the Company, but of the community at large; was a good soldier, is a good Sergeant, and will make a good Captain or Colonel. Stood face to face with the Rebels at Elmira, and never evinced the slightest degree of cowardice.

He is the junior partner of the firm of F. Brooks & Son, so favorably known throughout the county. The most fastidious cannot fail in being exactly suited with a selection from their extensive assortment of hats, caps or furs.

P. L. ROOT, Painter, enlisted May 12th, 1863. Served but a very short time.

ERASTUS M. CRONK, Traveling Agent, enlisted May 19th, 1863. Mr. Cronk's profession is such that necessarily he is absent from many of the drills and meetings of the Company, but he is always willing to pay for all such absences.

He procured a substitute that represented him in the United States army, with a desire to do all that he can for the good of the organization, and a perfect willingness to stand by all rules and regulations of the Company. He is a good member, although only occasionally meeting with them.

DeWitt Guard.

E. T. GARDNER, Mason, enlisted May 19th, 1863. At the time the Company volunteered in the service of the general government, Mr. Gardner *did not* go, being under eighteen years of age at the time he enlisted, and not legally a soldier. Hence his name was stricken from the Roll.

E. M. GREENLY, Professor in Ithaca Academy, enlisted May 20th, 1863. Very much of the time since his enlistment he has been traveling in foreign countries. Since his final return he has not renewed his membership.

WILLIAM H. HERN, Clerk, enlisted May 21st, 1863. Mr. Hern was a first-class soldier, and a young man of high standing and great respectability in society. He removed from this village to the city of Syracuse; is engaged in candy manufacturing. Has also a large bakery which is in opperation day and night, and is doing a very profitable business.

THOMAS HERN, Confectioner, enlisted May 21st, 1863. Served with the Company in the United States army, and was a true and faithful soldier; was respected by both officers and men.

ALBERT PRAME, Shoemaker, enlisted May 21st,

1863. Is now Corporal, which position he gained by being one of the most regular members at meetings and drills, and one the best drilled soldiers of the Company. Corporal Prame is one of the most unassuming and quiet members, but one of the best men that ever kept step with the beat of the drum. He proved himself one of the "excelsior" during the term of enlistment in the United States service. Was one of the guard over a large detachment of troops sent to the front, and we speak understandingly when we say he was the best soldier that possibly could have been selected for that purpose. No bribe, however large, was sufficient to induce him to depart from his duty in the slightest degree. He well and truly performed all the duties required of a soldier, and was honorably discharged with the Company on expiration of his term of enlistment at Elmira.

CHARLES R. RANDOLPH, Book-Binder, enlisted May 21st, 1863. Is brother of the late Major John Randolph. Served with the Company until transferred to the 50th Regimental Band, by order of Colonel Henry D. Barto. Mr. Randolph furnished a substitute to represent him in the army of the United States, after paying three hundred dollars, being one of the original drafted men.

Mr. Randolph is Foreman in the Bindery department of the establishment of Andrus, McChain & Company. Has not only the confidence and respect of his employers, but of the community at large.

E. E. WARFIELD, Harness-Maker, enlisted May 21st, 1863. A good soldier, an honest, upright man, and a superior mechanic. Was with the Company at Elmira, and honorably served the full term of his enlistment.

CHARLES RICE, Rail Road Man, enlisted May 21st, 1863. But never served.

WILLIAM S. CRITTENDEN, Clerk, enlisted May 21st, 1863. Mr. Crittenden is a good member, and is faithfully serving the term of his enlistment. Was with the Company in the United States service, and performed all the duties required of him. Is a book-keeper and accountant; and has been selected as the most competent person to take the militia enrollment of this district.

URI CLARK, Jeweler, enlisted May 26th, 1863. Sergeant Clark is as good a soldier as he is a perfect engraver, and as good an officer as he is skillful and perfect in the various arts of which he is master. With no show of arrogance on account of his attainments, he fulfills his duties as a member of the DeWitt Guard as cheerfully and as consistent as he does any and all the duties of a good citizen, and an upright member of society. He was honored by the members of the Company by being elected in the first place to the vacancy occasioned by the promotion of the fourth Corporal; he bore his honor meekly, and by gradual promotion has reached the rank of third Sergeant.

Sacrificed his business for the sake of doing his duty as a soldier, and volunteered with the Company in the service of the United States in September, 1864, and most honorably did he serve the full term of his enlistment.

E. C. MARSH, Merchant, enlisted June 3d, 1863. Served honorably as Lieutenant in the United States army. We have been unable to procure his war history for publication.

W. H. HOYT, Tobacconist, enlisted June 3d, 1863. Furnished a good and acceptable substitute to represent him in the army, for which he paid one hundred dollars. Is engaged largely in the manufacture of cigars. All who appreciate a good cigar, and who indulge in this luxury, should try the brand manufactured by our friend Hoyt.

L. P. KENNEDY, Merchant, enlisted June 9th, 1863. We envy no man his task were he compelled to find, in this lower sphere, a more consistent, upright and generous man, or a more devoted, faithful and exemplary soldier, than Corporal L. P. Kennedy; always at the drills, invariably present at all parades, and never absent at the meetings of the Company. He was represented in the United States army by a good and faithful substitute.

He is engaged in a general dry-good and fancy trade, and is receiving a liberal share of the public patronage.

E. M. LATTA, Turner, enlisted September 2d, 1863. Corporal Latta is one of the members that the Company, and all who feel an interest in its welfare, are greatly indebted to. One of the most punctual and regular attendants at all the meetings, drills and parades; so much so, that it is the remark of those present, when the Corporal is absent, that something serious is the matter. A finer soldier never shouldered a gun, a perfect gentleman, a splendid mechanic, and a citizen respected by all who know him. One of the best shots in the Company, invariably taking a prize at the target shoots. He volunteered and was mustered in the United States service with the Company in 1864. No more faithful or better soldier ever swore in the service, always ready to do any thing he was called upon, and many times did double duty to relieve others whom he thought not as well able to perform the labor as himself. The attachments formed by members of the Company while at Elmira, will long be remembered, and the name of Corporal Latta will stand high upon the list of those who rendered many kindnesses, and was always so willing to do any thing for his comrades that would tend in any way to meliorate their condition. He was detailed several times and sent with detachments of troops to the front, and in all his trips never lost a man. Served the full term of his enlistment and was honorably discharged.

JOHN SHAW, Student, (date of enlistment not recorded). A very active member; joined the Company when a mere boy and filled the position of marker. As soon as he was of suitable age and size, he shouldered his gun and became a regular member; he served well and faithfully until he left his home to attend college.

We believe it is his intention to devote himself to the ministry.

M. G. PHILLIPS, Blacksmith, enlisted September 2d, 1863. Mr. Phillips was an honored and respected member, a good soldier, and a conscientious man. He died December 26th, 1864.

FRED. GREENLY, Student, enlisted September 2d, 1863. A young man of fine attainments, and a splendid soldier. He served with the Company as long as he was a resident of the place.

Is now a Professor in the Military Academy at Eaglewood, New Jersey. Received his first military education in this Company, and was under the instruction of Colonel K. S. VanVoorhees.

WILLIAM K. STANSBURY, Book-Keeper, enlisted September 2d, 1863. Served as marker in the Company until September, 1864, when he resigned.

FRANK PERRY, Confectioner, enlisted September 3d, 1863. Was a good member, and served faithfully until he removed from the district. Is now a resident of the city of Syracuse.

C. R. BALDWIN, Furniture Dealer, enlisted October 8th, 1863. Furnished a substitute who represented him with the Company in the United States service, for which he paid one hundred dollars. Is engaged in the most extensive Furniture trade of any establishment in the county.

JAMES PATTERSON, Cigar-Maker, enlisted October 8th, 1863. Served with the Company until he volunteered in the United States army. He was a good soldier, and received a number of promotions in the army. Was engaged in many battles, an account of which we are unable to give.

EUGENE E. BARNARD, Clerk, enlisted October 8th, 1863. Son of Professor M. R. Barnard, and nephew of John Barnard, the hero of Lookout Mountain. By reason of his superior qualifications as a soldier, was honored by being elected Corporal, which office he now holds, and fulfills the duties required of him as such with perfect satisfaction. He volunteered with the Company in the U. S. service, and served his full time with honor. Was most a capital fellow in camp; always performed his duty well, and was honorably discharged with the Company on the expiration of their term of service. The Company can ill afford to lose Corporal Barnard.

JOHN C. CLEVELAND, Furniture Dealer, enlisted October 8th, 1863. Served but a short time.

LINUS S. MACKEY, Painter, enlisted March 5th, 1864. Mr. Mackey was a good soldier, as may be inferred from the fact of his promotion from the ranks of this Company to Sergeant of the Engineer Corps of the 50th Regiment.

He enlisted in the United States army August 6th, 1862, at Ithaca, and attached himself to Company D, 143d, New York Volunteers; was soon promoted to Sergeant. He served in the army until September 16th, 1863, at which time he was honorably discharged, by reason of disability from disease of the lungs contracted while in the army.

M. M. BROWN, Physician and Surgeon, enlisted March 7th, 1864. Doctor Brown joined this Company out of pure patriotic and christian motives, supposing that the government would accept the services of the Company when offered, which offer was twice tendered the government during the short time he was connected with the Company. Believing that they were not to be called upon to defend the honor and integrity of the country, the Doctor furnished an acceptable substitute, and was, by reason of his profession, relieved from further membership. The Doctor is engaged in a very successful practice in our village and is one of the Coroners of the county.

STEPHEN F. LEWIS, Artist, enlisted June 7th, 1864. Mr. Lewis is most an acceptable member. Is temporarily absent in the city of New York perfecting himself in his favorite art. He served with the Company through the Elmira campaign, and was a true soldier.

We hope our comrade will soon be again with us.

THEODORE DESCHNER, Gun-Smith, enlisted June 22d, 1864. Mr. Deschner was originally from Danzig, Prussia Proper; was engaged five years in the Prussian service; was promoted from the ranks to a non-commissioned line office, and again to Captain, and served as such from 1848 to 1850. He received a severe wound while bravely charging with his men in a sharply contested fight in the Province of Posen in 1849. From the effects of this wound Mr. Deschner has never recovered, and will, in all probability, be a sufferer during life. In 1850 he was engaged against the Austrians. In 1854 he was again called into the service of his country, but suffering so acutely from his wound he resigned his office and came to this country and located in the city of Rochester, where he resided seven years; here he organized a Rifle Company. Finally upon the urgent solicitation of a number of citizens of this place, he removed here in 1861, and has been engaged in the manufactory of Guns and Pistols. He has the reputation of doing the finest work of any mechanic engaged in his branch of trade in the State; constantly receiving orders from the Eastern States, and his Western customers have not forgotten him. Has constantly on hand an extensive assortment of Guns, Pistols and Fishing Tackle.

Very soon after joining the DeWitt Guard, he was chosen Company Standard Bearer; later was appointed by Colonel Barto Regimental Gunner. Has been for the last three years Company Armorer, and all who have visited the Armory, and at all examined the guns and accoutrements, can testify to his qualifications for this office. He is probably one of the best, if not the best, marksman in Tompkins County, always taking a prize at the target shoots of the Company.

Mr. Deschner is a very worthy, upright and honest citizen, and is well entitled to all the honors that have been bestowed upon him.

WALTER C. STEEL, Student, enlisted June 22d, 1864. Mr. Steel is a young man that commands the respect and esteem of all his acquaintances. He enlisted in this Company as musician, but he is at all times ready to perform any duty in a military way that he may be called upon to do. He is not only an expert with the drum, but few can excel him in the tactics, is perfectly familiar not only with all the calls with the drum, but can go through the drill equally well. He volunteered in the United States service with the Company, and well did he serve out the whole of his time; ·of all the musicians at Elmira none could compete with Mr. Steel. He is a young man of much promise, and the whole Company wish him great success in whatever profession he may adopt.

GEORGE R. WILLIAMS, Vice-President Merchants' & Farmers' National Bank, of Ithaca, enlisted July 13th, 1864. For a perfect sample of an honest, upright, conscientious, as well as active, energetic and successful young man, we produce Mr. Williams. Notwithstanding his official duties, he endeavors to be present at the drills and meetings, and is an invaluable member. He volunteered in the service of the General Government with the Company in 1864. They were soon deprived of his services, by reason of his being detailed as chief Clerk at Head-Quarters. He however remained with them in camp, frequently volunteering to appear with them on dress-parade and during inspections. No man stood higher, or commanded more respect in Elmira, than Mr. Williams.

H. E. SMITH, Clerk, enlisted August 29th, 1864. Discharged July 7th, 1865; served with the Company at Elmira.

T. H. GRIFFITH, Miller, enlisted September 1st, 1864. A particular favorite with all the members at Elmira. Was Company cook, and no man could make army rations taste better than our friend Griffith. He served as a member until some time after the Company returned from Elmira, when, on account of his residence being in another district, he was honorably discharged.

H. L. MILLER, Farmer, enlisted September

1st, 1864. Harley was well liked by all the men at Elmira—and withal he was a first rate soldier. Although a resident of another district, is still connected with the Company.

J. W. BROWN, Clerk, enlisted September 1st, 1864. Brother of M. M. Brown, M. D., whose substitute he was. Served faithfully with the Company through the Elmira campaign; was a good soldier, and a young man of much promise.

CHARLES R. SHERWOOD, Clerk, enlisted September ——, 1864. Charley was a good young man, and was just as good a soldier. Served the full term of his enlistment with the Company at Elmira. Upon his return, removed to the city of Buffalo.

MARTIN BESIMER, Student, enlisted December 26th, 1864. A good soldier and a very fine young man. Served with the Company until very recently, when he removed from the district.

AARON OSBORN, Clerk, enlisted February 27th, 1865. Mr. Osborn is one of the very best members at the present day; always present and always prompt to meet his dues and other obligations, and as a soldier is excelled by very few; as a citizen he is respected by all. He is connected with the large Boot and Shoe manufactory of C. Christiance & Son, of this village.

W. V. Wood, Farmer, enlisted February 27th, 1865. Discharged June, 1866.

W. H. Hall, Clerk, enlisted February 27th, 1865. Volunteered from the Company in the United States Navy.

Charles A. Phillips, Clothing Merchant, enlisted February 10th, 1865. Mr. Phillips is one of the most active members; is its present Secretary; every body likes Charley. Is one of the firm of A. Phillips & Sons, extensive Clothing manufactures. The large and increasing business of their House is their best recommendation.

D. N. Johnson, Book-Keeper, enlisted February 27th, 1865. Son of Captain Johnson and brother of E. K., whose history has already been noticed. One of the most respected and esteemed young men of the village. A good soldier and a good member of the Company. Is confidential clerk and book-keeper with Messrs. Seymour & Johnson, merchants and general dealers.

C. L. Taber, Clerk, enlisted April 5th, 1865. Charley is a first rate boy; just as good a soldier, and equally as good a member of the Company.

WILLIAM HATCH, Steam-Boat Steward, enlisted February 10th, 1865. Any person who has traveled the waters of Cayuga Lake, and not heard of Billy Hatch, and not regaled themselves with the luxuries provided by him, is probably the very one who would deny the existence of any such sheet of water, or would astonish us no more were they to deny their own existence. To confine ourselves to Mr. Hatch's qualifications as a soldier, however, would be more proper in this connection; but where a man is as good in one position as in another, we are frequently apt to digress from our subject.

The time he is obliged to be away from the drills and meetings, he makes up by doing for the Company very much in other directions. One of the most prompt, as well as one of the most generous members, has frequently paid fines and dues or other obligations of other members, who he thought could not afford to pay for themselves. Although at many of our drills we miss Mr. Hatch, still he is a member we should be as unwilling to have leave us, as would Captain Wilcox, Captain Goodrich or the traveling community at large, to have him resign his position on the Kate Morgan.

M. J. BARKER, Express Clerk, enlisted May 4th, 1865. A very stirring and energetic young man, and a soldier of ability. Is properly appreciated by the Company he represents.

CHARLES F. CLARK, Clerk, enlisted May 4th, 1865. Is a young man of promise, a good soldier and first-class salesman. Is employed in the large dry-goods house of J. S. Granger & Company.

GEORGE POLLAY, Carpenter, enlisted February 1st, 1865. Served with the Company through the term of their enlistment in the United States army. Was there a good soldier; was discharged from the general service with the Company, and discharged from the Company soon after.

FRANK LUCAS, enlisted February 1st, 1865. A short time thereafter was discharged. Has served in the United States army.

GEORGE M. KING, Student, enlisted May 31st, 1865. A perfect gentleman, and as good a member as ever enrolled himself with the DeWitt Guard. He joined with a full determination to become as good a soldier as there was in the Company. He has applied himself most thoroughly, and we leave for those who see the Company on parade to judge how near he has reached the goal of a soldier's ambition. Is a very fine shot, and has taken prizes at the various target practices.

WARREN H. LEWIS, enlisted June 7th, 1865. Soon after left to seek his fortune in the oil regions of Pennsylvania.

CHARLES W. CONOVER, Farmer, enlisted June 7th, 1865. Although Mr. Conover has belonged to the Company but little over a year, still by strict attention, and a determination to learn, he has become a soldier of merit. No member is more regular, or manifests a livelier interest in the Company than he. A stranger to many of the members when he enlisted, but soon he gained their well wishes, and to-day no one stands higher in the estimation of the Company than Mr. Conover.

FRANK BAKER, Farmer, enlisted June 7th, 1865. All that was said in relation to the last named soldier, is perfectly in place in this instance. Mr. Baker is a very attentive and active member; very few drills or meetings that he is not present, although he has further to come than any other person connected with the Company. Such members as these will in due time receive the promotion they have earned and are entitled to.

THEODORE J. SMITH, Cigar-Maker, enlisted June 17th, 1865. Mr. Smith is a good soldier, having served a long time in the United States service, a history of which we have been unable to obtain.

S. W. PURDY, Barber, enlisted June 20th, 1865. Was a much better barber than soldier; and although a sufficiently good marksman to take the first prize, still not generous enough to pay his Company obligations before leaving the place.

GEORGE L. CLAPP, enlisted June 20th, 1865. A fine young man and a good soldier, served his country during the late war. An account of his war history we have been unable to obtain.

FITCH R. CURRAN, Book-Keeper, enlisted June 20th, 1865. After a very short membership, our friend discovered that he had not yet reached the age of eighteen. Taking advantage of his age he withdrew.

JOHN F. YOUNG, Jeweler, enlisted June 20th, 1865. Mr. Young is a gentleman of much promise and an excellent soldier. Is one of the most active members of the Company. Is employed in the large establishment of Burritt, Brooks & Co., the oldest House of the kind in Western New York.

CHARLES E. FISK, Book-Binder, enlisted June 28th, 1865. Is one of the most respectable members at the present time, and is in all respects a fine young man. Is an employee in the establishment of Andrus, McChain & Co.

FRANK B. WYCKOFF, Clerk, enlisted September 6th, 1865. Mr. Wyckoff has been, and we hope will continue to remain, a good member of this Company, notwithstanding a little informality in his muster. Is employed in the Dry-Goods House of Morrison, Hawkins & Co.

M. B. APGAR, Turner, enlisted September 6th, 1865. Mr. Apgar was a fine soldier, and it was one of the misfortunes that the Company are constantly liable to, that he retired therefrom by reason of changing his residence to the city of New York. He was a United States soldier and was connected with Company G, 15th New York Cavalry. Was engaged in all the battles that the Regiment participated in. Enlisted at Ithaca, July 30th, 1863, and was mustered in at Syracuse, August 26th. He alone captured a number of prisoners at the charge on Martinsburg, August 21st, for which he was promoted to Corporal, and November 9th was again promoted to Sergeant. Was taken prisoner December 21st, 1864, but was soon exchanged. Received the farewell address of General Custer, May 23d, 1865, and was mustered out soon after. We are sure Sergeant Apgar was engaged in over fourteen battles. He is remembered as one of the defenders of the country.

NORMAN JOHNSON, Jr., Carpenter, enlisted September 6th, 1865. Mr. Johnson served in the United States army, but we have been unable to procure his history for publication.

JOHN S. HULBERT, Painter, enlisted August 24th, 1865. Mr. Hulbert withdrew from the Company and was discharged soon after his enlistment.

He enlisted in Company D, 137th Regiment New York Volunteers, August 16th, 1862, and was with the Regiment until the capture of Atlanta, at which time he was detailed as wagon guard at Head-Quarters. Was mustered out of the service June 9th, 1865. Was engaged in the following battles: Chancellorsville, Gettysburg, Wauhatchie Valley, Lookout Mountain, Missionary Ridge, Ringold, Resacca, Dallas

Woods, Pine Knob, Kenesaw Mountain, South Mountain, Peach Tree Creek and Atlanta. Another of the brave soldiers who served our Union in the recent civil war.

S. L. BAKER, Tin-Smith, enlisted September 6th, 1865. Mr. Baker is respected by all the members of the Company; is always punctual at the parades, drills and meetings, and is an industrious and worthy young man. Is employed in the extensive works of Messrs. Treman, King & Co. Took the first prize at the July target shoot.

HARLAN HILL, Rail Road Agent, enlisted September 8th, 1865. Mr. Hill is the gentlemanly Ticket Agent at the Delaware, Lackawanna & Western Rail Road Depot in this village, a position which he fills with ability. Although not long connected with the Company, still he has well perfected himself in the tactics, and is a prompt and active member.

R. W. DODD, Cigar-Maker, enlisted October 4th, 1865. Mr. Dodd was one of the first soldiers that enlisted from this village. Joining Company A, (Captain Jerome Rowe) 32d New York Volunteers. He well and faithfully served the full term of his enrollment, and again re-enlisted. We regret being unable to give a full history of Mr. Dodd's military life.

THEODORE QUICK, Cigar-Maker, enlisted October 12th, 1865. Mr. Quick has succeeded in perfecting himself as a soldier to a degree that but few attain. Few men can excell him in the tactics. Is an invaluable member of the Company. He enlisted in the United States army August 11th, 1862, in Company I, 109th Regiment, and served with the Company and Regiment until they were mustered out. Was engaged in the battles of the Wilderness, Spotsylvania, Petersburg, Welden Railroad and a number of lesser engagements.

On account of illness contracted in the army, was three months in the hospital.

W. S. MANDEVILLE, Clerk, enlisted October 12th, 1865. Considering the time he has served Mr. Mandeville is one of the best soldiers we know of, prompt, energetic and capable, we think, of commanding a Company or a Regiment. Immediately upon joining the Company, he manifested an interest, and with a determination to learn he attended every drill, and aside from this would by himself study the tactics, until he became perfectly posted in the science of military. He is a young man of much promise, and is the exemplification of a perfect gentleman. Is employed in the large Drug Store of Messrs. Schuyler & Curtis, and enjoys the confidence and respect, not only of his employers, but of the whole circle of his acquaintances, and the very many patrons of the House with which he is engaged.

J. J. MITCHELL, Merchant, enlisted October 12th, 1865. Mr. Mitchell beareth the same similarity to the last named member, that one pea beareth to another. As long as he was a resident of the village he was invariably present at the parades, drills and meetings of the Company. He is now a citizen of Lansing, but retains his membership in this Company, and meets with them on all parades. He is engaged in the Dry-Goods trade at Ludlowville, and is probably doing the greatest amount of business of any house of the kind—outside of the village of Ithaca—in Tompkins County.

CLARK FRALICK, enlisted October 5th, 1865. He enlisted July 20th, 1862, in the United States army, in which he served three years in Company D, 143d New York Volunteers; was engaged in six battles; was not sick a day while in the service, nor ever lost an hour from his Regiment.

E. M. THOMPSON, enlisted October 10th, 1865. Mr. Thompson removed from the place soon after his enlistment.

W. H. BROWER, enlisted October 31st, 1865. Signed the Roll, but never appeared at a meeting or drill.

E. G. FOSTER, Boat-Builder, enlisted November 6th, 1865. Soon removed to Minnesota.

LUKE BERGIN, Tailor, enlisted November 10th, 1865. Manifests but a slight degree of interest in the Company.

ARCHE DRESSER, Harness-Maker, enlisted November 10th, 1865. Soon removed from the district. Was a soldier, and a good one, in the United States army.

B. ALMY, JR., Teacher, enlisted January 17th, 1866. Mr. Almy joined upon transfer from the Enfield Company, of which he was Orderly Sergeant. Is a teacher of ability; his present engagement is with the Public School in this village.

JOHN E. CLAPP, Clerk, enlisted March 15th, 1866. Is one of the most attentive members at the present time.

H. G. STODDARD, Clerk, enlisted March 29th,

1866. Mr. Stoddard, as will be observed, has very recently joined, but promises to become one of the best members of the Company.

J. H. WILLETTS, Student, enlisted May 7th, 1866. Mr. Willetts joined the Company almost a perfect stranger to all the members, but by his gentlemanly deportment and perfect willingness to learn, has gained the respect of both officers and men.

M. McCALLESTER, Farmer, enlisted May 7th, 1866. His residence is so far from the village that he is only occasionally present at the drills and meetings, but from the eagerness he displayed to learn when he first became a member, we are led to believe he will make a good soldier.

C. N. TABER, enlisted May 31st, 1866. Mr. Taber promises to become a soldier of extraordinary merit.

LEWIS S. NEIL, Painter, enlisted May 31st, 1866. Although next to the last soldier enlisted in the DeWitt Guard, we are led to believe will soon become next to the best in his knowledge of military; and perhaps in this instance as in others, the last shall be first.

JOHN BARNARD, "The Hero of Lookout Mountain," seized with a patriotic ardour to serve his country in its trying period for National existence, on the 20th day of August, 1862, he volunteered and joined Capt. J. H. Terry's Company, then being formed in this village. Was duly examined and mustered into the United States service at Binghamton, N. Y., on the 25th of September, 1862. Was unanimously elected 8th Corporal of Company D. He left Binghamton with the Regiment for the seat of war, September 27th.

He accompanied General Geary on a reconnoissance to Manchester, which occupied five days. December 10th ordered to reinforce General Burnside at Fredericksburg. This was the first time our hero came within hearing of the enemy's guns, but his courage was equal to any emergency, and never, through the whole course of his military life, did he turn his back to the enemy, but always stood up and boldly battled for the right. Sunday, December 28th, had the first skirmish. On the 18th of January, 1863, was detailed by Colonel Ireland as one of the color guard of the Regiment. On the 27th day of April, was ordered on a march, and with eight days' rations and ninety rounds of ammunition, started for the Chancellorsville battle ground, where he arrived and participated in the battles of May 1st, 2d and 3d. July 2d and 3d were engaged with the enemy upon the bloody fields of Gettysburg. September 24th, was ordered to reinforce General Rosecrans at Chattanooga, Tennessee. October 29th, participated in the midnight battle of Wauhatchie. In this engagement one out of every three of the whole number were either killed or wounded. Color-bearer Baker was seriously wounded, and the colors of the Regiment fell into the hands of our gallant Barnard, he having escaped unharmed, although his overcoat, which was strapped upon his back, was shot through by one of the enemy's bullets. After this engagement he was detailed as color-bearer of the Regiment, vice Baker wounded.

On the 24th of November was ordered to march flying light, with only one day's rations; participated in the famous "Battle above the Clouds;" climbing over rocks and fallen trees, our bold and daring Sergeant succeeded in planting the colors of his Regiment on the rebel works, amid a terrific fire from the enemy. Sergeant Brink, with the State colors, was shot down upon his right, and Corporal Foot, of the color guard, upon his left. For this brave and heroic deed, Sergeant Barnard received the thanks of Colonel Ireland, as well as of all the general officers. November 25th, was engaged in the battle of Missionary Ridge, and November 27th in the battle of Ringold, Georgia. January 4th, 1864, was ordered to Stevenson, Alabama. While here Sergeant Barnard was detailed by the Commandant of the Post and appointed Post-Master, a very responsible position, having the entire charge of the mail for over five thousand troops. This office he held until Sherman's campaign against Atlanta commenced, and in May he again resumed his office in the Regiment. Was engaged in the action at Resacca, May 15th, battle of New Hope Church, May 25th, battle of Pine Hill, June 15th, and continued skirmishing until June 21st, when he participated in the battle of Kolb's Farm. June 24th battle of Kenesaw Mountain; still continued skirmishing with the enemy, and drove them across the Chattahoochie River. July 20th was in the battle of Peach Tree Creek; also in the siege of Atlanta, and was among the first troops that entered the city, September 2d.

November 15th he started on the Georgia campaign, and participated in the siege of Savannah from December 11th until December 21st, when together with the color-bearer of the 102d New York, he hoisted the old flag upon the City Hall in Savannah. January 27th, 1865, started on the Carolina campaign. Was engaged in the skirmishes at Edisto River, Lexington Court House, S. C., and Averysboro, N. C. Arrived at Goldsboro, N. C., April 1st, 1865. Was present at the capture of Raleigh on the 14th of April.

On the 30th of April, the war having virtually closed by the surrender of Generals Lee and Johnson, Sergeant Barnard, with his Regiment, started homeward, arriving in Alexandria, Virginia, May 19th. Took part in the Grand Review at Washington, May 24th, and on June 9th was mustered out of the United States service.

Sergeant Barnard was engaged in fourteen battles, besides numerous skirmishes, which, in times previous to the late war, would have been considered battles of much account.

Suffering all the dangers, exposures and deprivations of the Georgia and Carolina campaigns, our Sergeant was never a day from his Regiment, unless detailed for special duty. He made every mile of the whole march on foot, carrying a burden that every American soldier knows is enough to brake down the constitution of almost any ordinary man.

No soldier ever enlisted in the service of his country, who is deserving of more honor than Sergeant John Barnard.

Remember, you that staid at home and experienced none of the trials and deprivations of war, those who sacrificed their health, their lives and their all for you, as well as every other citizen of this great Republic.

HISTORY OF THE COMPANY.

The DeWitt Guard was organized in 1851, and the first regular meeting was held December 31st. At this meeting a series of By-Laws were adopted, very many of which are in operation at the present time, although there is not at the present time a single person connected with the organization who at that time was a member.

J. B. Terry was elected the first Secretary, and George H. Collins Treasurer, with Stephen Brewer and Loren Day as Directors.

At that time the law permitted the Companies to have a certain number of supernumeraries, and at the second regular meeting, F. Reed Dana, W. G. Maurice, Isaac Tichenor, Julius M. Ackley, Dana Fox, E. M. Marshall, John Rumsey, George McChain and S. B. Covert, were duly elected supernumeraries. The first out of doors drill took place in the Park, June 23d, and lasted two hours. The 4th day of July was duly observed by the Company; a parade, at which the Company did their first street firing, and a dinner at Colonel Seymour's Ithaca Hotel, constituted the festivities of the day. At the regular meeting, September 2d, 1852, a note was given to Colonel Millspaugh for fifty dollars, this being the amount he advanced to pay the Armorer's bill. On Thursday morning, September 23d, the drum beat at five o'clock, which warned the citizens of the near approach of the departure of Captain Partenheimer's Company, not for the seat of war, but for their first encampment at Goodwin's Falls. At 9 o'clock the life-like engine "Lackawanna," with a modesty becoming the Company to whom she belonged, introduced the Company to his honor "William E. Dodge," who safely landed his "precious load of freight" soon after at Goodwin's Landing. After a march of about three miles, to the music of Canham's Brass Band, the camp-ground was reached; tents were soon pitched, colors were hoisted, and at one P. M. were ready for our first rations; at two P. M. of the same day the Company paraded for the first time upon a camp-ground. The Company remained in camp one week.

DeWitt Guard.

Thursday November 25th, 1852, by proclamation of the Governor, was observed as a day of Thanksgiving. This being the day designated by the fair ones of our village for the presentation of the Banner to our Company, Captain Partenheimer's orders were responded to by a prompt and full corps. Upon being drawn up in line in front of the Clinton House, Hon. S. B. Cushing, on behalf of the Ladies, in a few appropriate remarks, presented the Banner. Our worthy Lieutenant Bruyn, on behalf of the Captain and his Company, returned his most sincere and heartfelt thanks, with a few remarks highly complimentary to him from whose hand he received the Banner, and to those Ladies instrumental in making the donation. After a parade through the principal streets, and giving each Public House a round of blank cartridges, with that good feeling ever manifested by the Company, they were dismissed by our commanding officer. March 3d William Glenny was elected Secretary in place of J. B. Terry, resigned.

July 4th, 1853, was duly celebrated by the Company by an encampment through the day in the Park. August 9th the Company were inspected by Brigadier General Segoine, of Auburn. September 8th, 1853, the second encampment of the Company took place at Goodwin's Falls; were here again reviewed by General Segoine and Colonel D. E. Avery. On Sunday the Company in a body attended church at Trumansburg. Washington's birth-day, February 22d, 1854, was observed by the Company; a national salute was fired by Sergeant McDonald, loading and firing five times a minute. June 27th the committee of arrangements for the celebration of the coming Fourth of July, offered the Company thirty dollars if they would participate in the celebration, which was promptly refused, and the Company voted unanimously to join in the celebration without money and without price. Accordingly the Fourth day of July, 1854, was duly celebrated in the true spirit of '76. The first target shoot of the Company was held July 11th, 1854, and resulted in Sergeant McDonald taking the first prize, L. Millspaugh the second and S. Stoddard the third. Saturday August 26th, 1854, the Company appeared in full uniform at $5\frac{1}{2}$ o'clock, A. M., to escort the remains of their late comrade, D. Lewis Avery, to their last resting place. His remains were taken to Aurora for interment.

Monday August 28th, the Company started for Camp Seneca, at Seneca Falls, where a week was spent by them very profitably. The second target practice was September 22d, 1854, and Sergeant L. R. King, E. C. Fuller, M. E. Elmendorf, Lot S. Hinds and Sergeant McDonald, were declared the best shots, and received the prizes accordingly. January 8th, 1855, was duly observed by the Company; in the evening had supper at the Clinton House. September 6th the Company unanimously voted to furnish uniforms free of expense to all new members who would join. September 14th, 1855, K. S. VanVoorhees was elected first Sergeant, L. R. King, second Sergeant, F. K. Andrus, third Sergeant, and James McClune, fourth Sergeant. September 19th, third target shoot, the lucky ones not recorded. October 31st, 1855, the Company were inspected and reviewed by General Segoine and staff, and Colonel D. E. Avery and staff; in the afternoon of the same day was another target shoot. November 29th the Company escorted the remains of their late Lieutenant, A. H. McNeil, to the Depot, being en route for the city of Auburn. The Company held their annual meeting and took supper at the Clinton House, January 8th, 1856. May 28th L. R. King was elected first Lieutenant, in place of W. V. Bruyn, resigned, and Charles F. Blood second Lieutenant, in place of A. H. McNeil, deceased.

Wednesday June 11th, 1856. The Willard Guard of Auburn, accompanied by Scott's Cornet Band of Rochester, arrived on an excursion to Ithaca. When nearing the dock they were saluted with twenty-one guns from the DeWitt Guard, and received by them accompanied by the entire Fire Department of the village, and were escorted through the principal streets to their quarters at the Clinton House. They were there welcomed by an appropriate speech from J. H. Selkreg, Esq. William Shapcott, of the Willard Guard, returning thanks on behalf of their Company to the soldiers, Fire Department and citizens, for the cordial manner in which they had been received. The Willard Guard paraded during the forenoon of the following day, and at five o'clock P. M. were escorted to the Park by the DeWitt Guard, where they were drilled in the different evolutions of military tactics with great credit to themselves. On Friday morning the DeWitt Guard again paraded and escorted their visitors to the Steam-boat Landing. After a few speeches, a great rivalry was kept up between the two Companies for the last cheer, but amid the clattering of drums it was impossible to tell which succeeded.

September 2d, 3d, 4th, 5th and 6th, the Company were encamped at Dryden; on Friday they were reviewed by General Segoine and staff of Auburn. The encampment passed off with perfect harmony, and without any thing to mar the good feeling which prevailed throughout. Tuesday, December 10th, the Company escorted the remains of their late member, Sergeant James C. McClune, to their last resting place. February 24th, upon invitation of the Pioneers of Tompkins County, the Company paraded and escorted that body through the principal streets of the village. September 15th target shoot. October 13th the Company were inspected at Goodwin's Falls by Adjutant George H. Collins. Upon invitation of the President of the Tompkins County Horticultural Society, the Company paraded and attended their Fair, June 3d, 1858. Upon invitation of the Tompkins Blues, the Company visited Trumansburg and joined in celebrating the Fourth day of July. A very pleasant entertainment was provided by the citizens of that place. July 21st the Company visited Owego, and were agreeably entertained by the citizens; returned the same evening.

August 17th, 1858, the Company paraded in honor of the *successful laying* of the Atlantic Cable. August 31st, upon invitation of the Ithaca Fire Department, joined with them in procession, and escorted Cayuga Hose Company No. 4, of Auburn, to the Clinton House.

"The DeWitt Guard, accompanied by Whitlock's celebrated Cornet Band and several invited guests, left Ithaca at 7 o'clock A. M., July 12th, 1859, on an excursion to our neighboring city of Auburn, and to enjoy one of the *pleasantest trips ever experienced* by any Company of soldiers. The Company mustered two Lieutenants, three color-bearers and twenty-five men. The smiles of Heaven seemed to be upon us, and every thing seemed given to *conduce to our happiness*. It was indeed a lovely sight as we floated down the beautiful Cayuga, which lay sleeping between the banks of those noble hills, decked in nature's verdant garb. It would have been a lovely scene for some artist to sketch in glowing colors; but no artist could touch so tenderly the points with which nature has adorned them.

We arrived in the beautiful city at half-past twelve, amid the thundering voice of artillery. Were received by the three military Companies of the city, and were escorted by them through the principal streets to our Head-Quarters, White's Exchange. After a capital dinner, we were marched to Fort Hill Cemetery to visit the grave of our lamented Lieutenant, A. H. McNiel; an hour was spent in that beautiful cemetery. In the evening we *were entertained* at the residence of Mayor B. F. Hall, which entertainment passed off to the perfect *satisfaction of all present.* Wednesday morning were called together at ten o'clock, and accepted an invitation of the Military Committee to visit the Prison and Insane Asylum.

In the afternoon the Auburn Companies, together with the DeWitt Guard, paraded for nearly two hours, after which each Company was practiced in the Battalion movements; the DeWitt Guard taking the lead. Each Company displayed a thorough discipline in military tactics, the movements being of almost mathematical precision. In the evening the Company were the guests of Doctor Willard, and was splendidly entertained at his beautiful residence on Genesee street. The Doctor is a model gentleman; truly did we enjoy his hospitality. From his residence we were marched to that of Captain Dodge of the Willard Guard, where a splendid reception was given in honor of the DeWitt Guard. Here we were honored with the society of some of Auburn's fairest daughters, their influence on us being such as (in the language of our worthy Chaplain, Rev. W. C. Steel) to make some *willing captives.* The Company returned late in the evening to their HeadQuarters, highly pleased with their evening's entertainments. Thursday morning the Company was marched to some of the principal residences, paying our compliments to those of whom we had been the honored guests the evening previous. The hour of two P. M. having arrived, the time for our departure, we were escorted to the Depot by the military Companies together with many citizens. Hon. A. Wells extending our thanks to the soldiers and citizens of Auburn, for the kindness shown us during our visit with them. Rev. Mr. Steel following in a few beautiful and appropriate remarks, during which tears were seen to fall from the eyes of some of the soldiery. We had won many friends; the hour of separation had arrived; nothing could be more expressive than the falling of a tear, the utterance of the soul, simple yet unexpressed; no language could be more eloquent. We entered the cars amid many cheers, having had proof that pleasures enjoyed excel pleasures anticipated.

After a pleasant return trip on the lake, we were much surprised to find our own good citizens in large numbers, together with a Company of Cavalry and the entire Fire Department, at the landing ready to receive us, and escort us to our homes. We were received with a beautiful and eloquent speech by Marcus Lyon, Esq., which was responded to by our Chaplain, Rev. W. C. Steel. Were marched through the principal streets to our Armory, highly pleased with our trip. Long will this excursion be remembered by the DeWitt Guard; our *hearts* having been united to the soldiers and *people* of Auburn by those bonds of friendship which time shall never efface." JOHN C. HAZEN, Secretary.

The 50th Regiment National Guard, consisting of Company A, Captain P. J. Partenheimer, Company D, of Trumansburgh, Captain Belnap, and Company I, of Havanna, Captain Mulford, the Regiment commanded by Colonel H. A.

Dowe, encamped at Ithaca, September 5th, 1859. On Friday were inspected by General Segoine, of Auburn, and Adjutant Van Voorhees, of Ithaca. The weather was fine during the encampment, every thing passed off pleasant and to the satisfaction of all concerned. Long will Camp Burnett be remembered by the members of the DeWitt Guard. January 4th, 1860, Colonel A. E. Mather was elected a member of this Company, but was never mustered in. June 4th, 1861, the Company paraded and escorted the Dryden Volunteers to the Depot.

July 3d the Company was presented with a handsome stand of colors by Sergeant John C. Hazen. April 2d, 1861, the Company tendered their services to the General Government. August 6th, 1862, escorted volunteers to the Depot; three hearty cheers were given by the members of the DeWitt Guard, for those of their number who had volunteered in the service of their country. September 28th attended the funeral of Lieutenant Marsh, at McLean, who was killed in the army. October 28th, 1862, were inspected at Trumansburg. December 3d Captain Blood introduced the Bayonet Drill. February 22d, 1863, was celebrated by the Company by a parade, and a supper in the evening at the Clinton House. March 19th attended the funeral of Peter J. Hausner, a soldier who died from disease contracted while in the army. June 17th, 1863, the Company the second time offered their services to the Government. June 22d the Company paraded in honor of the returning volunteers, and escorted them through the streets of our village. July 1st attended the funeral of Lieutenant Avery, at Farmerville, who was killed in the army. Celebrated the 4th day of July, 1863, by an excursion to Long Point, at which place the Company engaged in target practice with both muskets and artillery. Annual parade, inspection and review at Ithaca, October 21st, 1863. Were inspected by General William Glenny and Colonel H. A. Dowe, since promoted to Brigadier General. The Company had another target practice same day. Washington's Birth-day, February 22d, 1864, was celebrated by a parade and supper in the evening at Gregory's. April 25th, 1864, the Company for the third time offered their services to the General Government. July 4th paraded and had target practice. Aug. 28th, the Co. was accepted by the Gen'l Gov't for 100 days' service at Elmira.

(*By B. R. W., Secretary.*)

SEPT. 2d, 1864.—The Company assembled at the Armory at 6 o'clock, A. M., with tears in their eyes and carpet-sacks in hand, to march for Elmira. Headed by their gallant Captain, they proceeded silently to the Depot, where the parting was truly heart-rending, and the Secretary, in order to hide his feelings, was forced to take refuge in a freight car, and solace himself with a fresh chew of *Mike Wick's best*. The voyage was safely performed, the only cause of complaint being the *rye* treatment which some of the men received at Willseyville.

The grand entree at Elmira was made at about two o'clock, P. M., where we were received in behalf of the United States by the brilliant and dashing Captain Colby, of the 58th, by whom, assisted by Drum-Major Robinson's justly celebrated martial band, we were escorted to Barracks No. 1.

On entering the portals of this haven of rest, our ears were saluted with cries of *Fresh Fish*. Our inexperienced eyes searched eagerly on every side for this delectable delicacy, but we failed to discover it. The future movements of the Company at this post are recorded by our worthy Sergeant, H. S.

ELMIRA CAMPAIGN.

DETAILED ACCOUNT OF THE DOINGS OF COMPANY A,
FIFTIETH REGIMENT N. G., S. N. Y., WHILE PER-
FORMING ONE HUNDRED DAYS' DUTY
AT ELMIRA, NEW YORK.

Taken from the Diary of one of its Members.

———•♦•———

In pursuance of Orders as follows:

GENERAL HEAD-QUARTERS STATE OF NEW YORK,
ADJUTANT GENERAL'S OFFICE,
Albany, Aug. 28th, 1864.

SPECIAL ORDERS, No. 348.

Captain Charles F. Blood, commanding Company A, of the 50th Regiment National Guard of the State of New York, will, by the 5th of September, proximo, proceed with his command to Elmira, N. Y., and report to Major A. S. Diven, acting Assistant Provost Marshal General, and Superintendent of the Volunteer Recruiting Service, who will muster them into the service of the United States for one hundred (100) days, and attach them to the 58th Regiment National Guard, of the State of New York.

Requisition for the necessary clothing and transportation will be made upon Brigadier General S. V. Talcott, Quartermaster General, No. 51 Walker Street, New York city, and for arms and accoutrements upon Brigadier General James A. Farrell, Commissary General of Ordinance, State Arsenal, New York city.

By order of the Commander-in-Chief,
JOHN T. SPRAGUE,
Adjutant General.

HEAD-QUARTERS 50TH REGIMENT N. G., S. N. Y.
Trumansburg, N. Y., Aug. 27th, 1864.

SPECIAL ORDERS, No. 3.

Above Special Order, No. 348, is hereby promulgated.

Captain Charles F. Blood, commanding Company "A," of this Regiment, will immediately promulgate the above Orders to his command.

Said Captain will immediately report to these Head-Quarters, in writing, the strength of his command, and the number of men he will be able to report for duty at Elmira on the 5th day of September, proximo.

The Captain will see the importance of this Order, when it is stated that orders must be made at once for clothing, transportation, arms and accoutrements, at New York city for his command.

By order of
COL. HENRY D. BARTO,
Commanding 50th Reg't N. G., S. N. Y.

LEWIS HALSEY, Adjutant.

Company A, 50th Regiment National Guard, State of New York, started at 9 o'clock on the morning of the second day of September, 1864,

DeWitt Guard.

in obedience with the above order, with the following officers and men:

    CHARLES F. BLOOD, *Captain*.
    LEVI KENNEY, 1*st Lieutenant*.
    JOSEPH ESTY, JR., 2*d Lieutenant*.
    J. C. HAZEN, *Orderly*.
    C. C. GREENLY, 2*d Sergeant*.
    E. M. FINCH, 3*d Sergeant*.
    H. A. ST. JOHN, 4*th Sergeant*.
    B. R. WILLIAMS, 1*st Corporal*.
    URI CLARK, 2*d Corporal*.
    J. C. GAUNTLETT, 3*d Corporal*.
    ALFRED BROOKS, 4*th Corporal*.

Frank Betts,	E. K. Johnson,
E. E. Barnard,	J. McKinney,
J. W. Brown,	W. H. Kellogg,
F. Cheesbrough,	S. T. Lewis,
Wm. Crittenden,	E. M. Latta,
A. Dean,	J. Mandeville,
James Faulkner,	E. C. Marsh.
John Gay,	H. L. Miller,
M. L. Granger,	J. W. Norton,
T. H. Griffith,	C. L. O'Brien,
George H. Grant,	A. Prame,
S. J. Humm,	O. S. Perry,
T. Hern,	George Pollay,

W. C. Steele,   E. E. Warfield,
C. R. Sherwood,   Geo. R. Williams,
H. E. Smith,   J. V. Wilson,

We reached Elmira at 2 P. M. on the same day, and were immediately marched to our quarters at Barracks No. 1, afterwards called the Substitute Camp. At $3\frac{1}{2}$ P. M. we were mustered into the United States service as Company L, 58th Regiment N. G., S. N. Y., Col. R. P. Wisner commanding, and the same evening, on the requisition of our Captain, we drew the following articles of clothing, arms and equipments, to each man:

1 Woolen Blanket,   1 Canteen,
1 Rubber Blanket,   1 Spoon,
1 Overcoat,   1 Knife and Fork,
1 Blouse,   1 Cup,
1 Pair Pants,   1 Plate,
1 Cap,   1 Knapsack,
2 Pair Drawers,   1 Haversack,
2 Pair Socks,
1 Pair Shirts,
1 Pair Shoes.

The arms served us were of the Enfield pattern, known as rifled muskets, and were said to have been taken off of a rebel blockade-runner.

which, together with the necessary belts, cap and cartridge boxes, made as complete an outfit as were given to any of the men serving in our army for the preservation of the Union.

One can scarcely imagine the ridiculous picture our boys made as they tried on their new clothes, so generously given them by "Uncle Sam." Here in one corner you might see a six-footer striving in vain to induce a pair of pants, by hard pulling and stretching, to reach below his knees, but finding no virtue in perseverance, he seizes the coat and finds to his dismay the same difficulty with the sleeves that he found with the pants—namely, too short. As he sits studying over his misfortune, he is hailed by another fellow just his counterpart, hobbling across the floor with a pair of pants so long that they threaten to trip him at every step.

But, O, dear! Look at that perfect picture of despair; a fellow who at home wears a number five boot, trying to make a pair of number ten shoes stay on his feet. Presently, however, a man is found whose fortune has dealt to him a pair of "gun-boats" a size too small, immediately, with true yankee spirit, a trade is made, and each is satisfied that he has made the best of the bargain; so by dint of exchanges, garments are found to fit, which at first seemed as if they had been distributed by common consent, the smallest men to receive those intended for the largest, and vice versa.

But what ails that fellow over yonder? He looks as if he had lost his last friend, and never expected to have another. We rush up to enquire the cause of his discomforture, but our anxiety is turned into laughter, when we behold him who had been congratulating himself on making such a fine appearance in a suit of blue; brushing off the threads and dust, and picking up one thread which seemed to be very long, but only producing the more thread by the greater picking, our fine fellow finds that he has ventilated the entire side of one of his trowsers legs. Hark! the Orderly cries " fall in for rations;" although we may not yet be perfectly acquainted with all orders pertaining particularly to camp life, yet all seem to understand this one. With a good appetite after our fun, we start for the mess-house. Some hungry man behind us as we march along, hopes the beef stake will be tender, and the potatoes well done, while another hints he does not like eggs too hard boiled, and a third says he must have his rolls hot, and good butter to eat on them, or he don't care for any supper; while a fourth never eats pies, and so of course is anxious to find a good pudding awaiting his ravenous appetite. But misery me! what a smell! where does it come from? most certainly from the mess-house, no denying that. As we enter, every man immediately loses his appetite; but bound to face the music, we all sit down, place our cups and plates on the table, and await coming events. Presently there comes a man with a basket of bread, another with a pan of beef and a third with a pail of coffee. Waiter No. 1 very dexterously causes a huge chunk of bread to alight on your plate; waiter No. 2 makes a piece of beef perform the same evolution, and your cup is soon filled. Here is your meal, now make the attack. Our bread and butter man seems patiently waiting, although very pale, and is only aroused from his stupor by a neighbor asking him if he is not going to eat; he meekly answers, by saying he is waiting for some sugar and milk for his coffee. But all are soon satisfied, and we go back to our barracks, our poor beef-steak-and-potátoe companion feeling very much disappointed.

Our duty at the substitute camp was to perform the guard duty necessary to keep the men from escaping, and also to act as guard in taking men from this post to the front. This camp was used as a rendezvous for substitutes, to equip them preparatory to sending them to the army. The larger proportion of the men sent to this post seemed to be composed of the refuse of all society, whose entire aim seemed to have been to enlist and desert as often as opportunity offered. They were a lawless set of men, and it was only by enforcing the most rigid discipline, that they were kept within bounds.

When a squad of substitutes was to be taken to the front, one or two commissioned officers were usually detached, together with a compliment of non-commissioned officers and privates, sufficient to carefully guard against desertions on their way. Ordinary freight cars were used for transportation, into which were crowded from 35 to 40 men, allowing five men in each car as a guard. It was a shameful way of treating human beings, crowded together for two days with barely room to move in, and being required to assume all manner of positions at night in order to get a little rest. Although sufficient rations were purported to be issued for the journey, yet they never sufficed, and the men often suffered from hunger. Yet in time Baltimore was reached, where all the men were generally put into comfortable quarters for a day or so, and then placed on board transports to be taken to different points on the Potomac or James Rivers.

These transports were often condemned, or at least unsafe vessels in the employ of the Government, with no conveniences for the accommodation of the number of men crowded on them. The writer had the misfortune to be on one of these miserable crafts. On the night of Friday, Sept. 9th, we left Baltimore with 1100 men, en route for City Point, on an old condemned English emigrant steamer. We were 55 hours making the trip (more than twice as long as we should have been), and twice the vessel was turned to be run ashore, as she leaked so badly, and the pumps giving out for a time, it was feared by her commander the water might put out the fires under the boilers, and at no time could the old tub be kept on an even keel. There were only a few casks of water, and no provisions of any kind on board. The rations issued to the men on starting were all gone long before we reached our destination, and not a little suffering was experienced by the poor fellows for want of something to eat. This is but one of many instances in which one portion of the men in the Government employ were made to suffer by the neglect and ill-treatment of another portion.

But to return to our camp at Elmira. Our duties were about the same thing every day; doing guard duty when it came our turn for detail, with the diversion of an occasional squad to the front. This began to be an old story to us, and we had to use our best endeavors to get up some little excitement to break the monotony of camp routine.

On the afternoon of Saturday, Sept. 10th, orders were issued to our Regiment to move to Barracks No. 3, without delay. It was a rainy day, and all felt more like staying quietly in the barracks than like packing up and moving; yet go we must, and go we did. The last squad left at 8 o'clock in the evening. Tents, of which each Company had twelve, including one officer's wall tent, were pitched for the night, and all made themselves as comfortable as possible. In the morning, although it had ceased raining, it was very wet, and the nature of the ground made it very uncomfortable. We arranged our camp with a little more care, building a stockade of boards two feet high, on which we pitched each tent, and also making a floor on the bottom. Later in the season we provided each tent with either a camp-stove or fire-place, which made our quarters very comfortable, even in the severest weather.

We also built a cook-house capable of seating our entire Company, and furnished it with a good stove and such other apparatus as was necessary to carry on our culinary operations. We were indeed the envy of the entire Brigade, and it is undoubtedly true that by our own exertions we possessed the best *arrangement* for promoting our own comfort of any Company on the ground. We were enabled by our advantages to provide all the variety possible with the rations served us. There was hardly a day but we were supplied with some delicacy by the kindness of our officers, that was not on the regular bill of fare. Indeed, our Table d'Hote gained such a notoriety, that in less than two weeks we had some of the staff officers as regular boarders, and our worthy Colonel considered it quite an honor when we gave him a standing invitation to partake of any meal with us when he did not see fit to go to his boarding house—an invitation that he often accepted and seemed quite to enjoy.

Our principal duty at Barracks 3, or the rebel camp, as commonly called, although the correct name was Camp Chemung, was to guard the rebel prisoners confined at this post. Almost every day, however, men were detailed and sent off on extra duty. The prison was formed of a stockade built of boards 14 feet long, placed perpendicularly on a fence frame, having the posts on the outside, thereby giving a perfectly smooth surface on the inside, quite impossible to scale. There were two entrances to the enclosure, one called the Main Gate, which was placed on front, and was the principal means of entrance, the other was called the Rear Gate, and placed at the rear of the prison on the river bank. All around this stockade, four feet from the top, there was a platform and railing for the guard to walk on, with sentry boxes about 240 feet apart. Besides the guard "on the fence," there was a line of sentinels on the ground outside the stockade. During the day men armed with revolvers were posted at different points in the enclosure, and at night were formed into a patrol guard. This patrol walked around the entire enclosure about 15 feet from the stockade, there being an interval of three minutes of time between each man. The guard on the fence and those outside were relieved every two hours; the patrol was relieved every four hours. It was the duty of the guard to challenge any of the prisoners who were approaching the stockade, a second challenge was given if the first was not sufficient, and if they still persisted and were evidently trying to effect some means of escape, the order was to fire on them and give the alarm.

There were about 300 men detailed for duty each day. These consisted of eight commissioned officers, 32 non-commissioned officers, and 260 privates. This number was distributed to four different positions, allowing an equal number of officers to each, but the men were apportioned to each post according to the amount of duty to be done.

The guard was formed and reviewed each morning at 8 o'clock, preparatory to going on duty; the new guard usually relieved the guard of the previous day at 10 o'clock, and were kept on duty 24 hours. Each squad was under command of two officers, and was divided into three reliefs; these reliefs alternated with each other in a duty of two hours, thus allowing each man four hours' rest out of six.

The field officer of the day was accustomed to make a complete tour of the camp during the day, and usually visited each guard post at least once during the night. Whenever he was seen approaching any of the principal posts, the entire guard had to be turned out in order to be inspected and reviewed by him.

During the night, from 8 o'clock in the evening until 6 in the morning, every half hour was called by the guard on the fence, at the same time giving the number of each post and the word "All's well."

The prisoners were divided into companies, each company being under the charge of an officer detailed for that purpose. Roll was called morning and evening, at one of which the officer was required to be present and to make a daily report to the commandant of the post. Two meals per day were given the prisoners, one at

8 A. M. and one at 3 P. M. They were furnished with good, wholesome food, prepared in an immense cooking establishment. Each company marched to this house at the regular hours, and were served with their rations, going immediately back to their quarters to eat them.

Several large and commodious hospitals were provided for the sick, arranged with all possible convenience, and attended by a corps of competent Surgeons.

One might draw a grand comparison between the way in which our men were treated in the different prisons of the South, and the treatment of rebels at the hands of our Government. We who have seen the worn-out, hobbling rebel prisoner, go forth exchanged, after a few months' imprisonment, a strong and healthy man, cannot but feel the contrast when we see old friends, who, months ago were freed from Southern prisons, even now unable to stand the burden of any daily toil, and still wearing in their deep-lined faces the marks of past hardships. And when we think of those who once filled the vacant places in our homes and in our hearts, who might now be with us but for such hardships, we can reflect only with shuddering upon the treatment they have received, and feel grateful that we are at peace again. Verily, many a tale that we might tell were better left untold.

On the morning of Friday, Oct. 7th, one of the guard on the outside of the fence discovered a hole, through which it was evident some of the prisoners had escaped. The alarm was given, but it was too late. On investigation there were found to be 16 prisoners missing. They had made a tunnel about four feet under ground and sixty odd feet long, large enough to allow a man to crawl through. The night in which they made their escape was very dark and stormy, and taking advantage of this, they completed their excavation, crawled through, and were free.

This mode of escape was afterwards often tried, but the above is the only instance in which any reward was obtained for the great amount of work thus expended. A fellow put into practical operation one day a novel method of escaping. It was customary on the death of any of the rebels, to carry them to the dead-house; here the bodies were placed in coffins, marked, and a register kept. From the prison they were carried to the burial-ground, where the coffins were placed in long trenches, with a head-board marked to correspond with the register kept at the prison. One day one of the assistants at the dead-house arranged with one of his fellows to be placed in a coffin, and have the lid lightly nailed on. He was carried to the burial-ground, and unloaded with the other bodies. As soon as the cart drove off, our sharp fellow easily kicked the lid off and made good his escape.

Our camp life was beginning to be very monotonous. Each day the same routine was observed, and we were at our wit's end to produce some sort of amusement. We were provided, however, with the following incident which served us as a fund for some days: On the night of October 15th, all the camps being quiet, and no sound coming through the still night air, save the steady tread of the guard, or the hoarse, hollow cough of the prisoners, at 11 o'clock we were all suddenly aroused from our slumbers by the report of the alarm gun, the long roll soon followed and instantly the officers were out ordering the men quickly into line, each Company was marched on the parade ground on a double quick, the line soon formed and every thing was in readiness awaiting orders. Presently an orderly came riding up assigning to our Regiment a position, then quickly to another camp he went, and we started at quick time for our position, just as we set off the battery came thundering down the road, the bugle sounded, men dismounted, pieces were unlimbered, quickly loaded, and ready for action. From the opposite direction came more field pieces which formed a battery just in front of our halting place, then by us rushed a Regiment, and to us again came the orderly, and we were divided, one Battalion went in one direction and the other in another. Thus the different commands were manœuvred for about an hour, finally a rest being allowed, the men began to enquire if we had not been "sold," as it was evident there was no disturbance in the prison camp nor any signs of an outbreak. But no one could give a solution to the problem, until the next morning we found it was all done by our Brigade Commander, to see what reliance could be placed on the men in case of an emergency.

In pursuance of orders received a day or two previous, our Regiment, together with the entire

Brigade, started at noon of October 19th for the general parade ground, to take part in a Brigade review, it was an informal affair and only occupied two hours, it was a sort of preliminary or drill to fit us for a grand review to take place some time in the next month.

Messrs. Tolles and Burritt came over from Ithaca, reaching camp the morning of October 20th, to take views in and about the camps, they succeeded in getting a great many fine views of the different positions occupied by the troops.

At inspection on the morning of October 23d, orders were issued to each Regiment, to hold themselves in readiness to fall in at a moment's notice. It was understood that Governor Seymour was in the city and would visit the different camps during the day. It being unknown at what time we would have to fall in, our boys went about the camp with their equipments on, ready to take their places in line at the first call. In the afternoon at 3 o'clock the roll was sounded and our Regiment was soon in line, presently Gov. Seymour and a few members of his staff, accompanied by some of the post officers, passed and were saluted by the Regiment; there was no pretentious show of any kind, merely a recognition and compliment to the Commander-in-Chief of the State forces.

On the evening of October 24th, our boys arrainged one of their characteristic performances —a minstrel show. We had indeed acquired a great reputation during our life in camp for being possessed of an inexhaustable store of fun, and had the material for engaging in anything that might offer which could be turned into a source of amusement.

On the evening mentioned we built a staging of rather large dimensions of material furnished us by the Quarter-Master of the Regiment, sticking bayonets in the ground with a candle placed in them to serve as foot-lights, seats were provided for our audience, and every convenience added as far as possible in order to make our entertainments popular. We were richly rewarded on this occasion as our performances had been growing very much in favor, and on this night many came up from the city in carriages until we had an audience of which many a more worthy showman might have been proud.

It would be impossible to enumerate all the sources of fun that were introduced and carried out, but it is sufficient to say that there was not an hour in the day but that one might enjoy a hearty laugh over the pranks of one or more of the boys.

The 2d of November was a great day among the different Regiments stationed at Elmira. A grand review had been ordered to come off at noon, to consist of all the troops not on duty, to be reviewed by General Diven and staff. There were nine Regiments and two Batteries on the field, viz: the 12th Regulars, 1st V. R. C., the 54th, 56th, 58th, 77th, 98th, 99th, 102d Regiments N. G., the 4th Regulars, and Rochester Batteries. The line was formed at noon, on the large field in the rear of the regular parade ground. Soon after, General Diven and staff came on the ground, receiving the customary salute from the Batteries. We were marched in review, first at common time, then at quick time. After going through some minor evolutions, we were dismissed, reaching our camps just before 6 o'clock. Everything passed off well, and the reviewing officers expressed themselves highly satisfied with the appearance of the men, and their proficiency in drill. There were about 4,500 men of all grades, who took part in the review, and those who witnessed the parade considered it a fine affair, as well as being a creditable appearance of our State troops.

It was now drawing near the time when a great many of the Regiments were to be mustered out of service, having served the time for which they enlisted.

On the 3d of November the 54th Regiment was mustered out, and left for home. On the 5th, the 56th, 77th, and 99th Regiments were also dismissed from service, and each set out for their respective homes. This made our duties very much harder, as no troops were furnished in place of those leaving; consequently those who remained had to do double duty. We did not mind that much, however, as we knew our time would soon come for going home; although it would be near the middle of December before our 100 days were completed, yet our time was out with that of the remainder of the Regiment, who were mustered in some 20 days before we were.

The evening of November 16th was occupied by our Company in giving an oyster supper as a complimentary entertainment to the officers of the Regiment. The table was set and supper served in our cook-house. Among our guests we had the Colonel and staff, and nearly all the line officers of our Regiment, together with several members of other Regiments. Everything passed off finely, and both guests and hosts seemed to enjoy the evening's fun to the fullest extent.

It was fully expected by the authorities that the Regiment would be relieved from duty by the 20th of November, but all hopes of reaching home before the first of the following month were given up, for we certainly could not be spared until some Regiment should come to take our place, as there were barely men enough to do the duty required, and even those were virtually over-worked. It made little difference with us, however, as we had some time yet to serve, but then we had expected to be relieved from duty the same as the rest of the command to which we were attached, and felt some little disappointment at the delay. All were anxious to be home at Thanksgiving, the 24th of November, to eat the time-honored roast turkey and plum pudding, but we found it was of no use to raise any expectations, as they were not to be realized. We were not forgotten, however.

There arrived from home the night before several boxes and barrels, well filled with all the delicacies, as well as substantials, that are necessary to make up a grand Thanksgiving dinner. These were spread and partaken of by our boy with seemingly as much pleasure as if we had been at home.

After many disappointments and vexatious delays, orders were issued on the 1st of December to the effect that any Company having the proper papers drawn up and showing no deficiency as regarded equipments, should be mustered out on the 2d day of December, or as soon thereafter as all necessary papers were completed.

You may imagine that a great amount of writing was done during that night, as the next morning found us ready for the mustering officer. Quite early in the morning we began to pack up and make preparations to break camp.

At 10 A. M. the Captain was in possession of the Quarter-Master's and Ordinance officers' receipts for arms, accoutrements and camp equipage returned, and at 11 A. M. we were mustered out of the United States service, having been Uncle Sam's boys in blue just ninty-two days. We soon after set off for the Depot with what baggage we had, and at 7 P. M. reached Owego where we had to remain until morning.

At about 7 o'clock we were in sight of home and soon at the Depot, here we were received by a large number of citizens and marched directly to the Armory where we were welcomed home in a short speech by *M. R. Barnard*, neatly responded to by *Captain Blood*, after which we separated to don a citizen's attire and citizen's employment.

Although our three months' work, in the mere point of dollars and cents, was a loss to every man, yet I doubt if there is one who regrets having spent this much time in the government service. Each man received a regular discharge which in years hence he may refer to with somewhat of pride at the thought of having done even his mite in serving his country and contributed a little towards suppressing the rebellion. We were regularly enlisted in the United States army, and subject in every particular to the same treatment and usage as any of the men in the government employ. Our duty, it is true, was not attended with any of the dangers which accompanied the duties of the men in the field, yet it was work that had to be done, and could be as well performed by State troops as to take veterans from the field. Our Company as a whole were well treated in every instance, enjoying many advantages which the social position of the members secured to them, and we were allowed privileges which were hardly expected; in fact our standard of capabilites was raised so high that our men were constantly being detailed for some special duty, requiring men of more than ordinary intellect and foresight to accomplish. Soon after moving to Barracks No. 3, two of our men were detached from the Company and placed in the capacity of chief Clerks at Brigade Head-Quarters, another was made Clerk and Assistant to the Post Inspector, each retaining his responsible position during our stay in camp. Another was appointed to the position of Ordinance Sergeant, while a fifth member held the rank of Sergeant Major for a number of weeks, during the absence of the regular occupant of that office. Any one at all acquainted with the duties devolving upon an occupant of either of these offices, may judge of the honor extended our Company, and the preference shown its particular members, by the appointments to such positions of responsibility and trust.

It may be a fact worthy of mention, that there was not a duty imposed on our men that was not promptly fulfilled; every detail called for was forthcoming, and that, too, without hesitation or caviling, which was so common among a large number of the Companies. This is the more noticeable, as during the last few weeks of our stay at Elmira our boys were called on to do double duty. There were so many of the Regiments going home, and no provision made for supplying their places, yet every duty was cheerfully performed, although some men did 40 hours actual duty out of 48.

Every man had a pride in keeping everything in and about our quarters scrupulously clean. Our cook-house, with all its cooking apparatus, presented the appearance of a model kitchen, and each tent was swept and arranged with all the care that could have been taken by a tidy house-wife.

In appearance and proficiency of drill, as a Company, we soon attained a place second to none, and which we easily retained against all competitors.

Through the exertions and faithfulness of our officers, we had the pleasure of receiving from

Captain Carpenter, the Post Inspector, the compliment that we were finest in appearance, and most proficient in drill, of any of the Companies stationed at Camp Chemung.

Our officers were ever watchful to promote the comfort and best interest of the men, striving in a hundred different ways to lighten the duties imposed on the men, providing everything in their power to relieve the sick, besides, at a personal expense, contributing many articles of food or camp furniture, so that, by their exertions, the irksomeness of our duties was destroyed, and every man considered it more of a pleasure than an obligation to obey their commands.

We were sorry to part with many of our own Regiment, as well as members of other commands with whom we had formed an acquaintance, much to our profit, but our work had been done, and we were honorably discharged, returning home feeling that the time had been well spent, and with no regrets that we had been in the United States service for three months.

December 26th a delegation of the Company attended the funeral of M. G. Phillips, a late member. January 5th.—Annual meeting and supper at Captain Esty's. Washington's Birthday, February 22d, 1865, was duly honored by the Company by a parade. May 28th—Attended the funeral of the late Lieutenant George Fisk. June 27th—Were inspected at Trumansburg by Colonel H. D. Barto. July 7th—A number of members were expelled for violation of By-Laws. Attended the funeral of Captain Bartholemew, at Etna, who was killed in the United States service. August 3d—Attended the funeral of Major Belcher, who died from disease contracted while in the army of the United States. Target shoot August 15th, 1865. The prizes were taken and awarded as follows :

1st. William S. Crittenden—a splendid Revolver, presented by Captain Esty.

2d. Walter C. Steel—a pair of rich, gold-lined Silver Goblets, presented by Lieutenant John C. Hazen.

3d. L. S. Mackey—a beautiful Silver Castor, presented by the Sergeants of the Company.

4th. Sergeant E. M. Finch—an English silver-steel, pearl handle Pocket Knife, presented by L. R. King, Esq.

5th. Geo. R. Williams—bottle of French Perfumery, presented by Geo. E. Halsey, Esq.

6th. John Young—a magnificent box of Herring, presented by J. B. Taylor & Co.

7th. Geo. M. King—a Glass Pipe, presented by Messrs. J. B. Taylor & Co.

After the prizes were awarded, Captain Esty was presented with a magnificent sword, belt, sword-knot and case, by Capt. B. R. Williams, on behalf of the members and ex-members of the Company.

The Company was reviewed and inspected by Colonels H. D. Barto and K. S. VanVoorhees, at Trumansburg, Oct. 19th, 1865. January 23d, attended the funeral of Chief-Engineer Joseph Sidney, U. S. N., who died while in the service of his country.

We now come in the history of the Company to the dedication of the new Armory and Drill-Room, which are located in the Cornell Library building, and which were dedicated by one of the finest entertainments ever given in Ithaca, February 10th, 1866, at which time the Company were assisted by Miss Louise St. John, Mrs.

J. S. Granger, Miss A. McCormick, Mrs. Joseph Esty, Jr., and Miss Frankie Atwater; also Gen. H. A. Dowe, Gen. William Glenny, Col. Charles F. Blood, Col. K. S. VanVoorhees, Capt. B. R. Williams, Quar. Mas. J. C. Heath, Hon. B. G. Ferris, Hon. James B. Taylor, F. M. Finch, Esq., F. K. Andrus, Esq., Charles Curtis, Esq., Edward Hall, Esq., Thomas Crane, Esq., Edward Moore, Esq., L. V. B. Maurice, Esq., Elijah Cornell, Esq., and Master Fred. Summers.

The entertainment was liberally patronized by the citizens of Ithaca, enabling the Company to cancel a large proportion of the indebtedness incurred in furnishing their Armory. The expenditures of the Company in this direction, and expense attending their exhibition, was six hundred and twenty-eight dollars and fifty-four cents.

The present indebtedness of the Company is less than two hundred dollars, which amount they hope to cancel entirely by the profits on the sales of this History.

The furniture of the Armory will compare, we think, with any room in the Library. A fine photographic likeness of each of the officers of the Company, taken by the celebrated Artists, Messrs. Beardsley Brothers, occupy a prominent position. The Drill-Room is one of the finest in the State. For the present superior advantages enjoyed by the Company, they are much indebted to Hon. Ezra Cornell, whose name is connected with every enterprise which has in view the prosperity of our village.

We have endeavored to give, as we stated at the commencement, a full, true and concise history of the DeWitt Guard, our task is completed; and in closing, we only ask that a generous public will remember the present and former members of this Company, who sacrificed so much for their country in the hour of her peril, and to bestow honor where honor is due.

www.ingramcontent.com/pod-product-compliance
Lightning Source LLC
Chambersburg PA
CBHW032137160426
43197CB00008B/672